Early Ye Placem

A Critical Guide nd ng Work-based l

 Jackie Musgrave
Nicola Stobbs

EARLY YEARS

First published in 2015 by Critical Publishing Ltd
Reprinted in 2015

British Library Cataloguing in Publication Data
A CIP record for this book is available from the British Library

ISBN: 978-1-909682-65-8

This book is also available in the following e-book formats:

MOBI ISBN: 978-1-909682-66-5
EPUB ISBN: 978-1-909682-67-2
Adobe e-book ISBN: 978-1-909682-68-9

Cover and text design by Greensplash Limited
Project Management by Out of House Publishing
Printed and bound in Great Britain by 4edge Limited, Essex
on FSC accredited paper

Critical Publishing
152 Chester Road
Northwich
CW8 4AL
www.criticalpublishing.com

Meet the authors

Jackie Musgrave is a senior lecturer in the Centre for Early Childhood at the University of Worcester. She qualified as a sick children's nurse and then taught early childhood care and education at a college of further education. She has taught higher education students for the past ten years. Jackie gained her Master's degree at the University of Sheffield, her dissertation focusing on an aspect of practice-based learning for level 3 students. Her thesis for her doctorate examined the effect of chronic health conditions on young children's inclusion in their early education.

Nicola Stobbs initially trained as a primary school teacher, teaching across various age groups. She then worked in an early years setting for 12 years as the setting manager. During that time, Nicola mentored many students on placement in her setting and also completed her MA in early childhood and gained Early Years Professional Status. Having combined her early years role with university tutoring for two years, Nicola then became a full-time lecturer at the University of Worcester. She remains committed to supporting students in becoming the excellent practitioners that children deserve.

Acknowledgements

Our grateful thanks to the students who have generously shared their experiences and provided contributions to this book.

We would also like to acknowledge our use of Crown copyright material which is gratefully reproduced free of charge under the terms of the Open Government License.

Dedication

This book is dedicated to our husbands and children.

Contents

Glossary   vi

1   Introduction   1

2   Preparing for placement   4

3   Becoming a professional in practice   15

4   Safeguarding   27

5   Key documents   36

6   Your first day   50

7   Linking theory to practice   57

8   Observation, assessment and planning   69

9   Statutory assessment   81

10   Working with colleagues   87

11   Working with parents   96

12   Relationships with children   104

13   Reflecting on and writing about placement   113

Appendix 1: Teachers' Standards (Early Years) September 2013   124

Appendix 2: Self-assessment audit of skills and knowledge   127

Index   133

Glossary

Children's centre	Place that offers multi-agency services for child development including the third sector (volunteers and charities).
CPD	Continuing professional development
Critical friend	Trusted friend who can provide support and give constructive criticism.
CV	Curriculum Vitae – a résumé of your professional experience and qualifications.
Development Matters	Non-statutory guidance material that supports practitioners in implementing the statutory requirements of the EYFS.
DBS	Disclosure and Barring Service: the service that makes police checks to identify whether people have a criminal record. It is a statutory requirement that people who are working with vulnerable people, such as children, are screened. If they have convictions for criminal activity, they may be barred from working with vulnerable people.
DSO	Designated Safeguarding Officer: the designated member of staff in an organisation for staff to go to if they have a concern about safeguarding. The DSO is screened and trained to be able to conduct this role and will have up-to-date knowledge of referral routes.
Early Years Teacher	Recognised qualification in parallel with existing Early Years Professional.
ECEC	Early Childhood Education and Care
ECM	Every Child Matters
Emotional Intelligence	The capacity to be aware of, control, and express one's emotions, and to handle interpersonal relationships judiciously and empathetically: 'emotional intelligence is the key to both personal and professional success' (Oxford English Dictionary).

EYE	Early Years Educator
EYFS	Early Years Foundation Stage: the Statutory Framework, which comprises of a set of welfare and learning development requirements that must be followed by providers who care for children between 0 and 5 years of age. The EYFS became statutory in 2008 and there were two revisions in 2012 and 2014.
EYITT	Early Years Initial Teacher Training
EYTS	Early Years Teacher Status
IEP	Individualized Education Program
Mentor	Trusted advisor (possibly tutor or lead professional) who has experience in the early years, who is able to offer support and advice through reflection on work and practice.
Mentoring	Nurturing an individual's progression through a supportive, professional relationship with a mentor.
Multi-disciplinary	Using the input of several professional agencies at the same time.
Nutbrown Review	A review of childcare qualifications carried out by Professor Cathy Nutbrown on behalf of the government.
NCMA	National Childminders Association
Ofsted	Office for Standards in Education, responsible for inspections and grading of settings in line with the Early Years Foundation Stage.
Parents	Described in law to include biological relationship (mother, father) and any other responsible adult (carer) who has taken this role in a child's life.
Partnership with parents	Working relationship with parents/carers, which encompasses mutual respect and information sharing to promote equality and prevent unfair practice towards families and children.
PBL	Practice-based learning
Pedagogy	Theory and main beliefs of teaching children with regard to the nature of children's learning.
Practice	Work methods
Practitioners	Adults involved – in this regard – with caring and supporting young children's learning across a range of settings.

Reflective practice	Reviewing actions and outcomes to inform future practice.
SaLT	Speech and Language Therapist
Schema	A cognitive framework or concept that helps to organise and interpret information.
SCR	Serious case review
SEN	Special Educational Needs
SENCO	Special Educational Needs Co-ordinator
Setting	A place where children and parents can access children's services. These cover a wide range of places including children's centres, nurseries, pre-schools or playgroups.
Two year-old check	Statutory assessment which is part of the EYFS.
Te Whariki	New Zealand Early Years curriculum
UNCRC	United Nations Convention on the Rights of the Child
WBL	Work-based learning

1 Introduction

Work-based learning (WBL), sometimes known as practice-based learning or professional practice, is a vital component of vocational higher education courses. The skills and knowledge that you can gain from WBL can dramatically increase your employability. The focus of this book is to guide you as student practitioners on early childhood education and care (ECEC) courses through your WBL with the aim of enabling you to have an outstanding experience and maximise your future employability. This focus is especially pertinent because the early years workforce is becoming increasingly professionalised.

The Nutbrown Review has focused attention on WBL as a vital part of becoming an effective early years practitioner:

> *Practice placements are an essential part of training …. Students need to observe and work alongside practitioners whose practice is high quality … Only settings that are rated 'Good' or 'Outstanding' by Ofsted should be able to host students on placement.*
>
> (Nutbrown, 2012, p 7)

There was also a recommendation that students should '*be experiencing practice in a variety of settings … so that they can see different ways of working and learn from a variety of expert practitioners*' (p 21). Further emphasis on the importance of placements was stressed by the recommendation that this should take place in '*at least three different and appropriate settings, to last a total equivalent of a minimum of twenty percent of the total course duration*' (p 23).

Although some of you will have undertaken some WBL prior to beginning your course, many of you may regard the expectations of you as undergraduates as daunting as well as liberating. This is partly because you are expected to work as part of a team of practitioners rather than as a student under the direction of teachers or college tutors. Tutors will explain the activities that you are expected to undertake during placement, however, there may be little time to address individual concerns or cover all possible eventualities. In addition to addressing the needs of undergraduate students, this book will address those of you who are already graduates and are working towards achieving Early Years Teacher Status (EYTS).

About this book

Each chapter has a visual map, which signposts the content of the chapter, and an explanation of how the content links to the Early Years Teachers' Standards (that were published in September 2013). This book has been written in a way that incorporates our students' opinions and views, as well as advice from practitioners, in the form of *Dear Student* letters. The content of the letters is intended to offer you support by covering a range of subjects and issues relevant to WBL. Other features to help you understand the topic being covered include critical questions, case studies and critical reflections, as well as suggestions for further reading.

Chapter 2 includes a range of practical considerations for you to address ahead of starting your placement. The theme of the chapter is to help you plan carefully for your WBL so that you do your utmost to ensure that you have an outstanding experience.

Chapter 3 deconstructs the meaning of professionalism for student early years practitioners. It explains the concept and helps you to understand what it means to be a professional student.

Chapter 4 outlines the main points about safeguarding and child protection. It draws on the messages learnt from serious case reviews and focuses on your role in safeguarding children as a student in practice.

Chapter 5 summarises key documents that have formed government policy in recent years. The chapter content makes links to your practice and includes suggestions of how they influence your practice and how they can be used in your academic work.

Chapter 6 includes a range of practical guidance of what you can do to make a good impression on your first day. For example, how getting to know the routines straight away can reflect well on how you are viewed by your temporary colleagues.

Chapter 7 helps to define what is meant by 'theory' and explains how and what you can use to support theoretical understandings of your practice.

Chapter 8 emphasises the vital place of observation, planning and assessment in contemporary ECEC. The content explains in clear language the links between these three concepts. The content explains how observations are the key to knowing children and how, in turn, knowing children can help you to plan how best to manage children's behaviour.

Chapter 9 addresses the statutory assessment elements of the Early Years Foundation Stage (EYFS), including the two year-old check and the end of key stage profile.

Chapter 10 gives you some suggestions of how to manage relationships with colleagues when on placement. It addresses some of the difficulties that male practitioners can experience in a predominantly female environment.

Chapter 11 discusses some of the challenges associated with working with parents from your perspective as a student practitioner.

Chapter 12 explores the difficulties associated with student practitioner and child(ren) relationships. The content encourages you to acknowledge your own feelings in such relationships and encourages you to think about your responses to contradictory, and sometimes unethical, practices that you may encounter.

Chapter 13 helps you to explore the concept of reflective practice in relation to your WBL experiences. There are examples that you can adapt to help you develop your skills in this important aspect of ECEC.

Before the appendices is a glossary of terms and acronyms used in ECEC.

Our commitment

As a Registered General Nurse/Registered Sick Children's Nurse and a trained primary school teacher, we are committed to the practice and principle of WBL, having benefitted from this when we were student practitioners and then subsequently as we mentored students undertaking WBL in our institutions post-qualification.

This commitment, based on our personal experience rather than evidence-based research, was upheld as we moved into higher education and we became responsible for the preparation of early childhood studies students in becoming professional practitioners. As we planned programmes that included elements of WBL we struggled to find a theoretical framework to guide our planning for student preparation for placement. Therefore, we decided to gain students and practitioners' views of what they think all students need to know as they partake in this valuable learning experience. We hope that you enjoy your placements, and most of all we hope that you find this book useful.

Reference

Nutbrown, C (2012) *Foundations for Quality. The independent review of early education and childcare qualifications. Final Report*. Runcorn: Crown Copyright. [online] Available at: https://www.gov.uk/government/uploads/system/uploads/attachment_data/file/175463/Nutbrown-Review.pdf (accessed 1 December 2014).

2 Preparing for placement

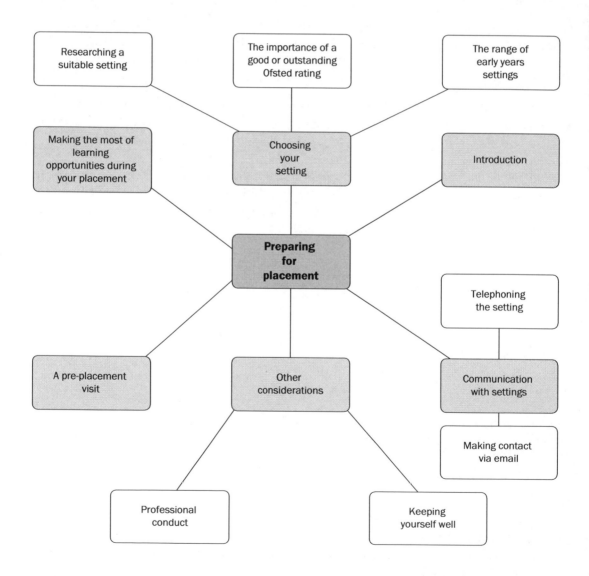

Researching a suitable setting

The importance of a good or outstanding Ofsted rating

The range of early years settings

Making the most of learning opportunities during your placement

Choosing your setting

Introduction

Preparing for placement

Telephoning the setting

A pre-placement visit

Other considerations

Communication with settings

Making contact via email

Professional conduct

Keeping yourself well

Teachers' Standards (Early Years)

The content of this chapter links to the following Early Years Teacher Award indicators:

8.1, 8.2, 8.3, 8.4, 8.5, 8.6 and 8.7.

Introduction

This chapter highlights some of the practicalities you need to consider when planning your professional placement or work-based learning experience. How well you plan will directly contribute to making your placement both useful and enjoyable. It is worth remembering that settings provide a placement on a voluntary basis and most practitioners are more than happy to invest time in mentoring students. However, you have an ethical responsibility to ensure that you are as professional as possible so that you make a positive contribution to the setting and, most of all, to the children's education and care. If you do not prepare well and do not have a professional approach, you are likely to divert practitioners' time away from the children in order to mentor you. Therefore, you have a responsibility to invest time and thought into this important aspect of your degree.

Choosing your setting

Universities have different approaches to how placement is organised and there are pros and cons to each approach. Whichever approach your university has, it is your responsibility to familiarise yourself with the guidance and do all you can to follow it.

Some universities may have a member of staff who is responsible for finding you a placement. It can be reassuring for you to know that someone else has this initial responsibility, especially if you have moved away from home to live at university. However, it may mean that you have little influence on where you go and this could be problematic in terms of how far you have to travel to get to your placement. On the other hand, your university may have a policy that expects you to find your own placement. If this is the case there will be support available to you from the university. For example, there is likely to be a named contact with responsibility for co-ordinating aspects of students' professional placements, even though they may not be responsible for allocating a placement. There may be a database of settings that the university works with in the near vicinity.

The importance of early childhood education and care (ECEC) means that there are many courses related to this subject and, therefore, there are many students seeking professional placement experience. It is a good idea to ensure that you find out the dates for your placement and start the process of finding a setting as soon as possible, so that you have a greater chance of being offered a place that best suits your objectives.

The range of early years settings

You may know exactly where you would like to work after you complete your degree and feel that going into practice in a setting that is different from what you want to do, or working with

Table 2.1 *The range of early years settings for professional placement*

Type of setting	Advantages	Disadvantages
Privately owned nursery		
Children's centre		
Pack away pre-school setting		
Childminder		
State-maintained nursery school		
State-maintained Reception class		
Private schools		
Special educational needs school or playgroup		

an age range that you do not want to work with in the future, is a waste of time. However, it is important that you take the opportunity to gain experience in different settings and with children across the age range. Doing so will help you to gain an holistic view of children's learning and development needs and this will be beneficial to you in gaining a broad understanding and knowledge of ECEC. You may also find that you enjoy another age group or setting far more than you expected. In addition, a broad range of experience will contribute to your employability. There are several settings for you to consider for your placement and Table 2.1 lists some of the options available to you. Use the table as a template to record your thoughts about the advantages and disadvantages of each setting for your career development. Start to keep a list of all of your professional experience so that you can include relevant details in your CV and/or job applications.

Critical questions

Using the list of settings in Table 2.1, think about government policy, the needs of children and families and consider the following questions.

» *Why is there such a range of early years settings available?*

» *Copy out Table 2.1. What are the advantages and disadvantages for children and families? Fill in the second and third columns of the table with your ideas.*

» *What are the advantages and disadvantages to your career development of spending time in professional placement in the above settings? Add your thoughts to the second and third columns of the table.*

The importance of a good or outstanding Ofsted rating

The Nutbrown Review (2012) emphasised the importance of professional practical experience for students. This is because it is vital that you learn from observing good practice so that you can develop your own good practice. Conversely, if you observe poor practice, it is possible that you will perpetuate this in your own practice. A measure of the quality of a setting is its rating from Ofsted (2014) inspections. As Chapter 5 explains, a recommendation of The Nutbrown Review is that students experience practice in a variety of settings (at least three) that have an Ofsted rating of 'good' or 'outstanding' (at the time of writing, 80 per cent of settings have been rated by Ofsted as good or outstanding). For this reason, it is important that you are in a setting with these ratings for your practice.

The exception to the recommendation that placement should be in a good or outstanding setting is if you choose to go and spend time with a childminder. There are requirements that childminders must meet if they wish to be on the Childcare Register. If they comply with the requirements, they will be issued with a certificate of registration by Ofsted. It is important that you check that a childminder has their certificate of registration available for you to see prior to starting a placement.

Researching a suitable setting

It will be necessary to research several practical aspects relating to your placement. If you are finding your own placement, you may need to do an internet search or use the university database, if they have one, to locate a setting that will offer you the kind of experience you are seeking. It is a good idea to select at least two settings that you think are going to be suitable. You can find out some useful information about settings by looking at their websites and also accessing their latest Ofsted reports.

Think about the following issues.

- How far away is the setting?
- Can you get there by public transport?
- Is there parking available?
- How many members of staff are there?
- How many children and what age ranges?
- Is the setting rural or urban?
- Have they offered placements before and if so for how many years?
- Does the setting provide mentorship for students?

Critical questions

» What do you think is your ideal setting and why?

» What are the advantages/disadvantages for your career development?

Communication with settings

Once you have an idea of where you would like to go, or if you have been allocated a placement, you will need to get in touch with the right person in the setting. Your first contact with the setting may be to ask if it is possible to work there as a student volunteer, or it may be to follow up the details you have been given by the university to make arrangements about starting your placement. Your university may advise you of the best way to approach your setting. Initial contact may be via telephone or email. You may find the idea of making a telephone call to somebody you do not know a daunting prospect, but it will be less so if you are well prepared. Jessica has written a letter giving her tips to help you make effective telephone calls with your chosen setting.

STUDENT VOICE

Telephoning the setting

Dear Student

Before I started my degree, I had hardly ever phoned somebody for a professional purpose. I was really overwhelmed at the prospect of having to do so. I was really nervous. I would have done anything not to have to make the phone call. In the end, I spoke to the tutor at uni and she told me that lots of students feel exactly the same. We had some time in a teaching session to discuss how to approach making contact with our settings. Having done this several times since, here are some suggestions of how to maximise getting a good response to the phone call.

Introduction and purpose of call

- *Introduce yourself and say that you are a university student and explain that you are hoping to spend some time on placement at their setting.*

- *Ask to speak to the person who has responsibility for student placements.*

Make contact with the student co-ordinator

- *Be really positive about the setting. If possible mention something that you know about the setting to convey that you have made an effort to get to know about them. You may be able to mention that another student had a good experience working there and this encouraged you to approach the setting.*

- *Have the dates of your placement available ready to give to the student co-ordinator. A common reason for not being offered a placement can be because the setting has already offered placements to other students. If this is the case, you need not spend time discussing the aims of your placement if they are not going to be able to accommodate you.*

- *Make sure that you have an explanation of why you are requesting a placement at the setting you are approaching. For example, if you need to gain experience working with babies, then make sure you are specific about where you would like to work. If you are clear about where you are hoping to work, it is more likely that you will avoid the frustration of not being able to achieve your aim.*

- *I have found that sometimes I have had to make several phone calls to organise my placement. I had to remember that practitioners are busy with the children and returning a call can be a lesser priority. I found that being polite and friendly and making comments to reflect my understanding of how busy they are was helpful. It is never helpful to get stroppy or upset about not having a call returned. I always make a note of who I have spoken to so that I can sound as if I really know what I am talking about when I phone the setting again.*

- *A student on my course had her placement cancelled a few days before she was due to start because there was a mix-up over the dates. So it is a good idea to confirm the dates in writing and ask for the email address to send it to.*

- *Whatever the outcome of the call, always be polite and thank them for their time and assistance. You never know when you might come across them again!*

Good luck with finding your placement!

Jessica

Making contact via email

If you make initial contact with your setting via email, you can use a similar approach. It is always worth investing the time in finding out the name of the correct person to send your email to if possible. Here is an example of an email you could adapt.

<u>For the attention of the student co-ordinator</u>
My name is Josh Hill and I am a second year student at the University of _____.
As well as being a student on the early childhood degree, I am also an Early Years Teacher Status trainee.

I have a two week block placement coming up starting on Monday _____ and ending on Friday _____. As part of my EYTS training, I need to spend some time in a Key Stage 1 setting. One of my student colleagues worked at your school last semester and she speaks very positively about the school. In particular, she learned a lot about the teaching of maths in KS1, which is an area I am interested in and need to know more about.

I would be very grateful if you would consider offering me a placement for these two weeks.

I hope that it will be convenient for me to phone you at the end of the week to find out if you think this is possible.

Perhaps you would be kind enough to email me back and let me know a good time to phone you, as well as the best number on which to contact you. In the meantime, if you wish to contact me, my mobile number is _____.

I look forward to hearing from you.

Yours sincerely
Josh Hill

When you have specified a time to make a call, it is professional to do your very best to make sure that you keep to the arrangement and don't miss the opportunity to speak to the correct person. Consider putting a reminder on your phone or an alert on your computer.

A pre-placement visit

If possible a pre-placement visit is a good idea to familiarise yourself with both the place and the people.

STUDENT VOICE

Hannah

My university encourages students to make a pre-placement visit. This has always been really helpful and I would advise you to make sure that you do this. It helps to reduce the stress of wondering what placement is going to be like, but more importantly, it helps you to appear professional and committed.

Visiting the setting before your official start date gives you the chance to make sure you can find your way there. When you make your pre-placement visit, you may not be travelling at a busy time of day, so make sure that you ask staff about rush hour traffic so that you can allow extra time for your journey. During this visit, take the opportunity to find out useful pieces of practical information that will help you to fit in straight away and make the most of your placement. The setting may have a student policy and they may ask you or tell you much of what is outlined in Table 2.2. You should ensure that you address the following issues during the visit.

Table 2.2 *Record of pre-placement visit details*

Issue to be discussed	Progress and/or details
Start and finish dates and times	
The names and key roles of practitioners in the setting: • manager; • room leader; • designated safeguarding office (DSO); • your mentor.	

Issue to be discussed	Progress and/or details
Ensure that you have evidence that you have your DBS details to give to your mentor	
Written information for you to give to the setting: • telephone/email details of contact at university; • letter to or handbook for mentor; • student report form; • attendance record.	
Show your list of tasks and work to be completed during placement	
Locate relevant policies: eg students on placement, health and safety and safeguarding	
What to wear during placement (uniform/own clothes/level of smartness?)	
Policy for reporting absence from the setting	
Sickness policy	
Use of mobile phones in the setting	
Arrangements for student breaks	

Other considerations

This section looks at some of the other considerations that are important for you to bear in mind while you are preparing for your placement.

Keeping yourself well

When you are working as a student in your placement, it is expected that you will make a full contribution to the setting. This can be exhausting. Therefore, it is important that you look after yourself so that you feel fit and healthy to give your best. You can keep yourself well by ensuring that you are doing the obvious things such as eating well and getting enough sleep. Less obvious ways of keeping yourself well are to do your best to minimise the chances of becoming unwell as a result of coming into contact with infectious diseases. You can do this by paying careful attention to hand hygiene and also by complying with health and safety policies in the setting, especially in relation to the management and disposal of bodily fluids.

It is unrealistic to think that all infectious diseases can be avoided and students often find that they catch a common cold or tummy upset when they start in a setting. If you develop one of these conditions you need to know what to do about attending the setting. If you get diarrhoea and vomiting, the setting policy will probably ask you to stay away from contact with children for 48 hours after your last bout of diarrhoea and/or vomiting to try to stop the further spread of the infection. The common cold is highly infectious and the most infectious period of a cold is during the sneezing phase, so ensure that you use a disposable tissue and take particular care to safely dispose of tissues and wash your hands regularly during this phase. A cold can make you feel very unwell for a short while, however, taking regular doses of suitable medication can help to reduce the symptoms of a cold. You may not feel as well as normal, but you should feel well enough to work.

It is also useful to check that you are up to date with immunisations, especially measles, mumps, rubella and pertussis (whooping cough). You can check your status by asking at your general practice and, if you are not immunised, this can be given to you and it may stop you contracting one of these potentially avoidable infectious diseases.

Professional conduct

At all times it is important to consider your level of professionalism and ensure that you are behaving ethically. Remember that your actions, whether positive or negative, impact upon the reputation of the university. While it may be obvious that you need to maintain confidentiality about information that you gain as a consequence of being in the setting, there are other less obvious factors to be aware of. A common problem that causes issues relating to professional conduct is the use of social media. Remember to exercise extreme care about what you post on social media sites. What you post will remain on your digital footprint. It is also worth remembering that as well as damaging your professional reputation, inappropriate use of social media can cause unimaginable damage to those who are targets of negative comments.

Another factor that can cause problems is if you come to realise that you have a pre-existing relationship with somebody at the setting – for example, a member of staff or members of a child's family. It is a good idea to mention this to your mentor as soon as you are aware of the situation. It is especially important if you think that there is potential for difficulties to arise as a consequence of the relationship. This means that you will have made a 'declaration of interest' and depending on the specific details of the relationship, you will be advised about what, if anything, needs to be done to avoid compromising your professionalism or damaging reputations.

CASE STUDY

Jo's pre-placement visit

Jo was making her pre-placement visit to the day care setting where she was going to be for four weeks. Her mentor, Sadie, was showing her around the tweenies room where Jo was going to be working. One of the children, a two year-old called Harrison, was crying, but when she saw Sadie he toddled over to her and put her arms up to indicate he wanted Sadie to pick him up. Sadie cuddled Harrison and quietly commented to Jo that the child's family was going through a difficult time and this had affected Harrison's behaviour in nursery. Jo realised that Harrison was the son of a neighbour for whom she had occasionally worked as a babysitter. Jo was not aware of any family difficulties, but she immediately realised that she could be in an awkward situation as a consequence of the overlap between her professional and personal life.

Critical questions

»   *What are the possible consequences if Jo does not declare an interest by telling Sadie of her relationship with Harrison and his family?*

»   *What are the possible courses of action to manage this situation?*

Making the most of learning opportunities during your placement

While you are on placement it is a good opportunity for you to gain a range of skills and knowledge related to the care and education of children in the early years. Appendix 2 at the end of this book gives a comprehensive list of required skills and knowledge relating to ECEC. You may wish to use the suggestions to audit your level of expertise and identify areas for development. Chapter 13 gives you more guidance on how to write and record your learning from your placement.

Critical questions

»   *How can you ensure that you maximise opportunities for learning in your setting?*

»   *How can you keep a record of the progress you have made in your learning during your placement?*

Chapter reflections

There is a lot more to think about and prepare for than you might have at first imagined. The more preparation and thought that you invest in this part of your practice, the more likely it is to be a really successful experience for you.

Further reading

Rose, R and Rogers, S (2012) *The Role of the Adult in Early Years Settings*. Maidenhead: Open University Press.

References

Nutbrown, C (2012) *Foundations for Quality. The independent review of early education and childcare qualifications. Final Report.* Runcorn: Crown Copyright. [online] Available at: https://www.gov.uk/government/uploads/system/uploads/attachment_data/file/175463/Nutbrown-Review.pdf (accessed 1 December 2014).

Ofsted (2014) *Childcare Register Requirements: Childminders and home childcarers.* [online] Available at: www.ofsted.gov.uk/sites/default/files/documents/eyfs2014/Childcare%20Register%20requirements%20-%20cm%20and%20hc%20from%20September%202014.pdf (accessed 1 December 2014).

3 Becoming a professional in practice

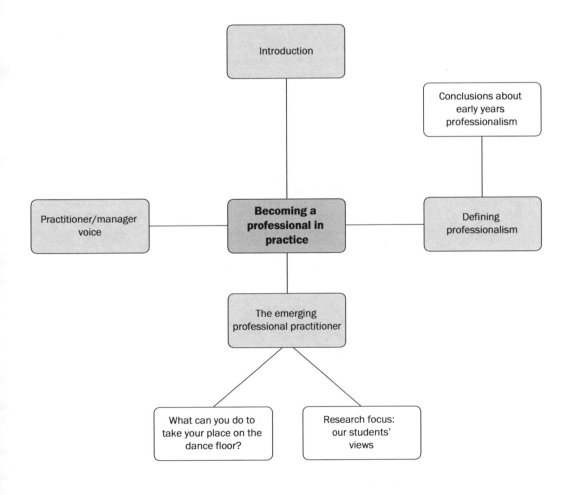

Teachers' Standards (Early Years)

The content of this chapter links to all parts of Standard 8 of the Teachers' Standards (Early Years): Fulfil wider professional responsibilities.

Introduction

The word 'profession' and the phrase 'being professional' are frequently used in relation to Early Years Education and Care (ECEC). However, definitions of these concepts are not always clear. This chapter unravels what these terms mean for students who are engaged in professional placements in early years settings. The chapter is structured into two main parts. The first part examines the status of the ECEC workforce and considers its current position as a profession. The second part considers what this means for you as a student working in settings on professional placements.

Defining professionalism

According to the Oxford English Dictionary, the term '*profession*' comes from an old English term meaning '*to declare publically*', so in a sense you '*profess*' to be skilled in a paid occupation, '*especially one which involves prolonged training and a formal qualification*'. The features highlighted in Figure 3.1 are frequently associated with an occupation that is regarded as a profession.

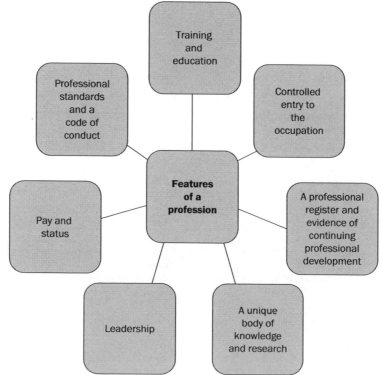

Figure 3.1 *Features of a profession*

Critical questions

»   *What type of occupations would you consider to be professions? Clearly doctors and lawyers are in this category, but what about footballers or cleaners? What criteria are you applying?*

»   *Consider the list of factors shown in Figure 3.1 and decide where you think the ECEC workforce 'sits' in relation to being a profession.*

»   *What other features might you include in a list of features for the early years profession? Explain your answers.*

The following sections explore each of these factors in relation to the ECEC workforce. As you read the sections, consider your role as a developing ECEC professional.

Training and education

We are living in exciting times for the early years workforce. It is currently going through a transition period from a workforce with minimal or no training and education, to one that is becoming highly trained with access to high level qualifications. Historically, the workforce emerged out of the tradition of older sisters taking responsibility for younger siblings while their parents worked. The sociology of childhood has changed over the past 50 years or so (see McDowall-Clark, 2013) and childhood is seen as a period of life that is distinct from adulthood. This change in children's roles has meant that in many countries of the world children are less likely to be expected to take responsibility for their younger siblings (although it is still the case in many countries).

Until recent times, childcare was not seen as requiring specialist knowledge or training. The first childcare qualification was created by the Nursery Nurse Examination Board (NNEB) in 1945, thus recognising for the first time that certain skills and knowledge are required to care for children. Nevertheless, childcare is sometimes viewed as an option that is (mostly) suitable for girls who do not have the qualifications for courses with higher entry requirements. This situation is changing, in part, for the following reasons:

•   increased awareness of the findings from neuroscientific research (see, for example, Gopnik et al, 1999) that indicated that the correct stimulation of the brain at the most opportune moment considerably enhances development;

•   a growing global awareness of the importance of children's early years experiences on their long-term development and potential.

Since 1997, there has been an increasing awareness of the importance of the education of children in the early years, as opposed to just care of children. David (2004, p 27) proposed that if we want our children to be *'brilliant, capable, strong and clever'*, then it follows that the workforce should also be brilliant, capable, strong and clever. Despite improvements, the current statutory guidance about qualifications is set unacceptably low. The Early Years Foundation Stage (EYFS) (DfE, 2014, p 20) states that *'in group settings, the manager must hold at least a full and relevant level 3 qualification and at least half of all other staff must hold at least a full and relevant level 2 qualification'*.

An important development in the professionalisation of the early years workforce was the introduction of the graduate level Early Years Professional Status (EYPS) in 2007. Professor Cathy Nutbrown's (2012) review of qualifications helped to highlight the importance of having highly qualified practitioners in early years settings. In response to the Nutbrown Review, *More Great Childcare* (DfE, 2013) was published and, as a consequence, EYPS was replaced by the Early Years Teacher Status (EYTS) qualification. The report set out the government's vision for improving the status and quality of the early years workforce. It stated:

> *The government wants to move decisively away from the idea that teaching young children is less important or inferior to teaching school age children. We want more high-quality graduates to work in the Early Years sector.*

> (p 7)

Also, in response to Nutbrown's recommendations, the National College for Teaching and Leadership (NCTL, 2013) created the Early Years Educator level 3 qualification. The first cohort started the qualification in September 2014. Applicants for the Early Years Educator need to have GCSEs in mathematics and English at a minimum of grade C. The effect of this requirement remains to be made evident, but it is a positive step to increase the educational standards of applicants joining the early years workforce. However, there is still a workforce with qualifications that range from a level 1 CACHE Award to a level 8 doctorate, and this variation in levels of qualifications and educational achievement of early years staff can have implications for undergraduate and postgraduate students in professional placement.

Critical questions

» *Imagine that you are a practitioner qualified to level 2 and you are allocated a third year, level 6 undergraduate student to work with you in the baby room. How might this make you feel? What potential issues could arise and how could they be dealt with?*

» *Now consider the situation in reverse – you are a third year undergraduate being supervised by a level 2 practitioner. How would this make you feel, what problems could arise and how might you address these?*

Controlled entry to the occupation

Partly because of the historical legacy of ECEC qualifications as outlined above, until recently there were minimal controls on who could enter the workforce. As a consequence, many practitioners did not (and some still do not) have basic qualifications in English and mathematics. However, as detailed above, this situation is changing and the EYTS mandatory requirement for a minimum level of qualification is a positive move towards restricting entry to the workforce to people who are capable of teaching the vital subjects to children using imaginative and playful approaches. *More Great Childcare* (DfE, 2013) states that:

> *Early Years teachers will be specialists in early childhood development, trained to work with babies and young children from birth to five. They will meet the same entry requirements and pass the same skills tests as trainee primary school teachers.*

> (p 27)

A professional register and evidence of continuing professional development

A feature of professions such as medicine and nursing is that there is a professional body that maintains a register of qualified practitioners. Fitness to practice can be defined as having the skills, qualifications and training to care for children to a high standard. An individual's eligibility to maintain their fitness to practice and thereby maintain their registration is demonstrated in two important ways.

1.   Individuals are required to conduct themselves within the law, although some traffic offences may not be viewed as seriously as other obvious crimes (see Chapter 4 for more about being a suitable person).

2.   Maintaining currency in your knowledge after qualifying is vital in order to be fit to continue to practice. Therefore, evidence of a practitioner's continuing professional development is required in order to maintain registration and eligibility to practice. For example, nurses are required to maintain their registration with the Nursing and Midwifery Council (NMC). They are obliged by law to keep a portfolio of evidence that demonstrates engagement with professional development.

At the moment, the ECEC workforce does not have an organisation such as the NMC. Therefore, maintaining a register and evidence of an individual's fitness to practice is not possible. This situation is one that needs to change in order to professionalise the sector and to help ensure that practitioners are suitable caring for, and educating, young children. However, the Standards for Early Years Teacher Status are an important landmark in professionalising the workforce.

A unique body of knowledge and research

A professional body develops its knowledge by conducting academic research. The findings from research are disseminated through publications and conferences. Historically, what we have learned about young children's development has been gleaned from a range of researchers from different disciplines. For example, Jean Piaget was a psychologist and he made a significant contribution to our understanding of how children learn. The legacy from him and many others has been vital. However, ECEC has become a robust academic community and the body of knowledge can be described as belonging to, and added to by, practitioners and academics. Consequently, in the spirit of multi-disciplinary and collaborative working, it is important that we continue to share research and learn from each other's disciplines, such as social work, health and psychology. An example of research that has added to the unique body of knowledge includes the work of academics who have researched the role of leadership in the early years.

Critical questions

»   *Do you think that replacing 'Early Years Professionals' with 'Early Years Teachers' will make the early years workforce more or less likely to be viewed as professionals? Why do you think this?*

» *How may the EYTS Standards help to professionalise the workforce?*

» *Maintaining evidence of continuing professional development is an important feature of professionalism of the workforce. Can you identify reasons why people may oppose this aspect of good practice?*

Leadership

There are many definitions of what is meant by leadership, but at its simplest, it can be defined as guiding or directing a group of people. It is not difficult to understand the importance of effective leadership for people serving in the military. The concept of leadership in early years used to be associated solely with management. However, this area has been researched widely by academics from a range of disciplines and it is now recognised that it is important for all practitioners, including students, to demonstrate strong leadership skills.

Pay and status

The historical legacy of the origins of childcare means that the workforce remains gender biased and has low pay and low status. This is partly because as people started to have smaller families and as more mothers returned to work, they had to look for out of home childcare arrangements. Some arrangements were informal. Childminding became an option for some mothers, partly because they could look after children in a homely environment. However, part of the attraction was that they offered low cost care. This started a trend of the public expecting low cost childcare, an expectation that is difficult to change when parents are responsible for meeting all of the costs.

The workforce has been left a legacy of low pay because of the previously held views that children simply required a watchful eye to keep them safe. In contrast, there is an emerging understanding of the knowledge, training and skills that are needed by the workforce in order to carry out the complex role of caring for and educating young children in order to promote their development and help them realise their full potential. This is especially true for children who are regarded as vulnerable. Therefore, it follows that the people who are dedicating themselves to such work should be rewarded with pay that reflects their skills and levels of expertise. The introduction of EYTS is undoubtedly an important step on the professional journey of the early years workforce, however, it is disappointing that EYTS does not include Qualified Teacher Status because this means that pay and conditions will remain much lower relative to the statutory school sector.

The issue of low pay is one that is being highlighted by the BERA/TACTYC (2014) *Policy advice and future research agenda* as requiring attention by the government. The document calls for:

> *Parity in pay and conditions between those who are teachers within schools, and those who are teachers in the Early Years sector, including the private, voluntary*

and independent (PVI) sector. This would be a major enticement to attract and retain high calibre staff in the Early Years workforce.

(p 2)

Professional standards and a code of conduct

Occupations that have been professionalised have a set of professional standards that have been created in order to guide the actions of people who belong to the profession. Nurses have a code of conduct that they are required to abide by. The EYTS standards (NCTL, 2013) state that Early Years Teachers (EYTs) *'act with integrity and honesty'* (p 2). This statement can be interpreted in several ways, but the intention is to convey that EYTs have a duty to be ethical in their practice. Most student practitioners will not be governed by the standards of the NCTL as EYTs are, however, this does not preclude you from demonstrating your commitment to practice with integrity and honesty. In other words, you are required to be an ethical practitioner. Being ethical involves causing no harm to others and this issue is explored in other chapters.

Conclusions about early years professionalism

The above sections have summarised the components of a profession and you may well have concluded that the ECEC workforce does not meet all of the requirements. There have been a range of positive developments, but there are still factors to be addressed, especially those of pay and status. The workforce can be regarded as an emerging profession and, of course, student practitioners can, and should, demonstrate professional attributes.

The emerging professional practitioner

This section explores your position as a student aiming to become a professional practitioner while gaining practical experience in a day care setting. Your experience will partly depend on the nature of the setting you attend. Wherever you spend your time on placement, you will be joining a well established team and you are likely to find this a challenging experience. It is not unusual for students to feel overwhelmed by the prospect of being an outsider. As is often the case, turning to theory can help you understand the process of making the transition from being a student on placement to becoming an emerging professional in practice. Wenger (1998) describes *'communities of practice'* and suggests that greater learning can be gained from becoming part of a community. In your case, it is important for you to become a member of the community in the setting where you are on placement. However, gaining membership can involve several stages. The following diagram draws on the views of several academics, including Wenger and Trayner's (2011) view of levels of participation (see Figure 3.2).

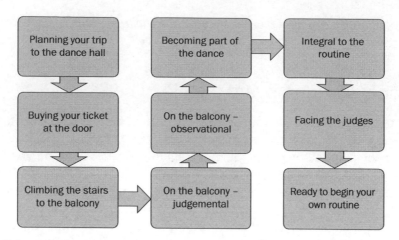

Figure 3.2 *Becoming part of the team (adapted from Wenger and Trayner's levels of participation)*

Professor Chris Pascal opened the 2012 BECERA conference by saying '*It's time to get off the balcony and onto the dance floor*'. Pascal's challenge to practitioners is that you join the dance floor; that is, be active in making a contribution to early years practice.

She was talking about engaging in practitioner research but it could also be applied to your attitude towards placement. You may have already made connections between this analogy and your own experience in placement. Imagine that you are interested in becoming a dancer. A national dance competition comes to your town and you decide to go along to the dance hall and buy a ticket. You climb the stairs to the balcony to view the dancers and on the way you notice things about the other people who are attending the competition, such as their ages. From the balcony, you watch the dancers on the dance floor, sometimes passing judgemental comments about the costumes they are wearing.

After watching and memorising the basic steps of the dancers' routine, you decide that you are ready to take your place on the dance floor. As you begin the dance you feel slightly self-conscious; it feels as if the eyes of all the dancers are on you. However, as you start to move with the music you remember how much you love to dance and soon you are integral to the routine, blending in with the professional dancers, instinctively knowing how to turn and twist. As the routine comes to an end you eagerly turn to face the judges, who ask what you would do if you were in charge of the dance next time, and you enthusiastically explain your ideas. After consideration, they pronounce that you have won the competition! Your prize is the opportunity to be the choreographer of the dance troupe and create a dance for an upcoming show. You are thrilled and leave the dance hall bursting with ideas to make the show one to remember.

RESEARCH FOCUS

Our students' views

In 2013, one of the authors of this book, Nicola Stobbs, collected the reflections of 70 early childhood undergraduates as they progressed on their journey to becoming professional practitioners. She then analysed their views and found that the students moved through several stages. The real-life comments shown in Table 3.1 can be related to the dance model above.

Table 3.1: Student comments supporting Wenger and Trayner's analogy

Student comment	Relation to analogy
'How should I contact my placement to make arrangements?'	Planning your trip to the dance hall
'I am going to have to do lots of work and it will be stressful'	Buying your ticket at the door
'It seems that the majority of practitioners are women'	Climbing the stairs to the balcony
'Some settings are disorganised'	On the balcony; judgemental
'There are many hierarchies in a setting'	On the balcony; observational
'How do I come across in practice?'	Beginning to dance
'How can I make an impact?'	Integral to the dance routine
'What do I consider a stimulating environment to be?'	Facing the judges
'How can I strike the right balance between free-flow and meeting learning outcomes?'	Ready to begin your own routine

The undergraduates experienced the feeling of 'getting off the balcony' when they realised that they had a part to play during placement. They recognised the chance to influence real children and families, rather than seeing themselves as outsiders observing from the sidelines.

Critical questions

» Consider where you are in the process in relation to your current placement. Where would you like to be?

» If you are not yet on the dance floor, what do you think you can do to help you gain your place with the team?

What can you do to take your place on the dance floor?

Most students have a valuable and enjoyable experience in their placement. However, some students have a miserable time and never manage to gain their place on the dance floor – that is, they do not become part of the community of practice. It is rarely a good idea to leave a placement early once you have committed to spending time with the setting, although there are some situations (see Chapter 6) where it may be the right decision.

The best approach to ensure that you do become part of the team as soon as possible is to prepare carefully for your placement. The suggestions of what you can do to improve your participation are summarised in the following letter, written by the manager of an early years setting.

PRACTITIONER/MANAGER VOICE

Dear Student

I remember with gratitude the teachers and practitioners who took time to coach me, sharing their knowledge and expertise. These mentors were supportive, but unafraid to give advice as well as praise. It is in this spirit that I write to you.

Never underestimate how much you can contribute to a setting. A common assumption is that settings are always pleased to have 'another pair of hands' but you bring so much more than merely being someone to help zip up coats and tie shoelaces. Your enthusiasm can lift the most melancholy of practitioners. You are up to date with the latest policy and teaching trends, which keeps us on our toes and reminds us that we should also be keeping up with our own continuing professional development. Your willingness to go the extra mile and give children extraordinary experiences helps prevent us from becoming complacent. However, there will be aspects of our practice that might not match your ideal and you should exercise caution when expressing this.

Imagine that you have a lovely home and you agree to let a stranger live with you for a week at your expense. At first the stranger is pleasant, but then begins to pass comments about the way you live: your bathroom taps are not as shiny as they would have expected; your children did not immediately go to bed when you asked them to. These observations may even be accompanied by an offer to help you sort out these concerns. How might this make you feel? Affronted perhaps?

You add to the emotional temperature of the setting, so draw on your emotional intelligence. If you normally 'tell it how it is', now is the time to show a little appreciation. You may feel intimidated by the experience of the other practitioners but they may well feel threatened by your 'expert eyes' judging everything they do.

You will endear yourself to them by getting down on the floor and playing with the children, not by giving them the benefit of your wisdom on how to improve the setting. So be humble, but not shy; if this is not you then 'fake it till you make it!' Your body language should say 'I'm professional, yet approachable'.

My advice to you is to look and see what needs doing and do it. For example, if a child spills their drink, get some paper towels and wipe it up. This will build a relationship of respect with the other practitioners and when you ask for your placement report it is less likely that there will be any nasty surprises.

Good luck on your professional journey,

Yours sincerely,

Setting manager

Critical questions

»   *How relevant to your experience do you consider the suggestions in the letter?*

»   *How easy or difficult would it be for you to achieve the suggestions? Explain your answers.*

»   *What could help you to do so?*

Chapter reflections

As the above sections have outlined, the ECEC workforce has made significant progress in professionalisation during the past ten years. This chapter has, first of all, attempted to examine the progress of the ECEC workforce on its journey to becoming a profession. Secondly, it has attempted to explain the theory that underpins the process of becoming an active member of the community of practice in your setting. Our research and the letter from a manager in a day care setting have provided several perspectives of what you can do to take charge of your placement experience right from the first point of contact with the staff in your setting.

Further reading

McDowall-Clark, R (2013) *Childhood in Society for Early Childhood Studies.* London: Sage.

Tomlinson, P, Davison, C and Waltham, S (2013) *Early Years Policy and Practice: A critical alliance.* Northwich: Critical Publishing.

References

BERA/TACTYC (2014) *Early Years: Policy advice and future research agendas.* [online] Available at: www.bera.ac.uk; www.tactyc.org.uk (accessed 1 December 2014).

David, T (2004) *Questions of Quality: The contribution of research evidence to definitions of quality in early childhood education and care practice.* Conference proceedings Dublin Castle, 23–25

September 2004. [online] Available at: www.cecde.ie/english/pdf/Questions%20of%20 Quality/Questions (accessed 28 February 2010).

Department for Education (2013) *More Great Childcare: Raising quality and giving parents more choice*. [online] Available at: https://www.gov.uk accessed (accessed 1 December 2014).

Department for Education (2014) *Statutory Framework for the Early Years Foundation Stage*. London: Crown Copyright. [online] Available at: https://www.gov.uk/government/uploads/system/uploads/attachment_data/file/335504/EYFS_framework_from_1_September_2014__with_clarification_note.pdf (accessed 1 December 2014).

Gopnick, A, Meltzoff, A and Kuhl, P (1999) *How Babies Think*. London: Weidenfield and Nicholson.

McDowall-Clark, R (2013) *Childhood in Society for Early Childhood Studies*. London: Sage.

National College for Teaching and Leadership (2013) *Early Years Educator (Level 3) Qualifications Criteria*. [online] Available at: www.gov.uk/government/publications (accessed 1 December 2014).

Nutbrown, C (2012) *Foundations for Quality: The independent review of early education and childcare qualifications. Final Report*. [online] Available at: https://www.gov.uk/government/uploads/system/uploads/attachment_data/file/175463/Nutbrown-Review.pdf (accessed 1 December 2014).

Wenger, E (1998) *An Introduction to Communities of Practice*. [online] Available at: wenger-trayner.com/theory/ (accessed 1 December 2014).

Wenger, E and Trayner, B (2011) *Levels of Participation*. [online] Available at: wenger-trayner.com/resources/slide-forms-of-participation/ (accessed 1 December 2014).

4 Safeguarding

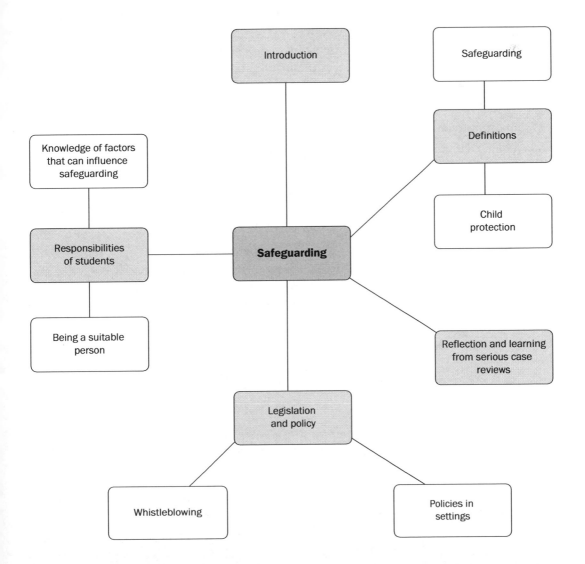

Introduction

Safeguarding

Definitions

Knowledge of factors that can influence safeguarding

Child protection

Responsibilities of students

Safeguarding

Being a suitable person

Reflection and learning from serious case reviews

Legislation and policy

Whistleblowing

Policies in settings

Teachers' Standards (Early Years)

The content of this chapter links to the following Early Years Teacher Award indicators:

7.1, 7.2 and 7.3.

Introduction

This chapter helps you to examine your role and outlines your responsibilities as a student practitioner in safeguarding children. Part of your responsibility is to understand the main legislation and policies relating to safeguarding children. In addition, you are encouraged to do as Munro (2008) urges us to do, which is to develop your ability to apply intuition and analytical thinking, in order to 'think outside the box' to keep the children you care for and educate safe. Unfortunately, even with rigorous statutory requirements, children can still die, or be harmed by those who are charged with caring for them. Looking at some of the recommendations from serious case reviews can help you to develop your awareness of safeguarding. This chapter will enhance your understanding of this critical area.

Definitions

It is important that everybody working with children understands the language of safeguarding as outlined in the *Working Together to Safeguard Children* guidance (Her Majesty's Government, 2013, p 85). The following definitions are taken from this guidance.

Safeguarding

Safeguarding and promoting the welfare of children is defined for the purposes of this guidance as:

- *protecting children from maltreatment;*

- *preventing impairment of children's health or development;*

- *ensuring that children grow up in circumstances consistent with the provision of safe and effective care;*

- *taking action to enable all children to have the best outcomes.*

Child protection

Child protection is part of safeguarding and promoting welfare. This refers to the activity that is undertaken to protect specific children who are suffering, or are likely to suffer, significant harm.

Therefore, child protection can be described as a response to particular concerns about a child who is thought to be suffering abuse and/or neglect.

Critical questions

» *Why is it important that you are clear about the difference between safeguarding and child protection?*

» *How can you work towards fulfilling your duty to safeguard and promote the welfare of children in your role as a student practitioner?*

Legislation and policy

Keeping children safe is central to the majority of people's aims, both as parents and as practitioners. However, the number of children who are harmed and sometimes killed, often within their own families, is of concern. Table 4.1 summarises the main policies from current safeguarding legislation.

Table 4.1 Summary of current policy aimed at safeguarding children

Policy	Aim
The United Nations Convention on the Rights of the Child (1989)	A global initiative stating that every child has the right to a childhood where they are safe from harm.
The Children Act (1989)	Placed the needs of the child as paramount and allocated duties to local authorities, courts, parents and other agencies to ensure that children's welfare is promoted.
Every Child Matters (2003)	The response to the Victoria Climbié Inquiry which aimed to improve services for children. ECM aimed to strengthen integrated ways of professionals working together.
Children Act (2004)	Required multi-agencies to form Local Safeguarding Children Boards (LSCB) with a responsibility for conducting serious case reviews (SCRs) in the event of the death or harm to a child.
Working Together to Safeguard Children guidance (2006 and 2013)	The guidance set out ways that individuals and organisations should work together to safeguard children. It emphasised that the child's needs are paramount.
Early Years Foundation Stage (2014)	Set out safeguarding and child protection requirements emphasising the need for the Designated Safeguarding Officer in settings to liaise with local statutory children's agencies and with the LSCB.

The government's *Working Together to Safeguard Children* guidance (Her Majesty's Government, 2013) makes it clear that '*safeguarding is everyone's responsibility*'. It also points out how all professionals have '*a role to play in identifying concerns, sharing information and taking prompt action*' (p 8). In order to achieve this aim, the guidance states that '*it is vital that every individual working with children and families is aware of the role that they have to play and the role of other professionals'* (p 8).

Policies in settings

The guidance also states that it is a legal requirement for early years providers to ensure that:

> *staff complete safeguarding training that enables them to recognise signs of potential abuse and neglect; and they have a practitioner who is designated to take lead responsibility for safeguarding children within each Early Years setting and who should liaise with local statutory children's services agencies as appropriate. This lead should also complete child protection training.*

> (p 50)

Settings must adopt the main points of the legal (or statutory) requirements and write their own safeguarding policies. It is vital that as a student you are aware of your setting's safeguarding policy and read it before starting work there and comply with the contents while you are on placement. Jacky's letter below (see Manager's voice feature) is an example of good practice in guiding students towards the safeguarding policy in her setting.

Whistleblowing

All settings and universities have a whistleblowing policy, which means that you have a responsibility to report any concerns you may have. You must ensure that you are aware of who is the Designated Safeguarding Officer (DSO) in your setting. If you are concerned about a safeguarding situation it is a good idea to write down your concerns straight away, with dates and as much detail as possible in order to remember the events with accuracy. It is also important that you discuss the issue with an appropriate member of staff at the university. If the situation involves a child's comments it is important to write down their words verbatim without asking any leading questions.

Reflection and learning from serious case reviews

Serious case reviews (SCRs) *'shed light on whether lessons can be learned about the way local professionals and agencies work together in the light of a serious injury or child death where abuse or neglect are suspected'* (Birmingham LSCB, 2013, p 1). There have been several high profile SCRs that have helped us to understand the complex influences that can compel people to cause harm to children. The following case studies highlight some of the main points that are pertinent to you as a student to reflect upon in relation to your role in safeguarding children.

Case study of Little Stars Nursery

The SCR that was conducted in Birmingham after a practitioner who worked at Little Stars Nursery was convicted of raping a child in the setting highlighted the actions of the students who were there on professional placement. The students became concerned about some aspects of practice in the setting and reported their concerns; their actions contributed to the practitioner being reported to the police. The SCR concluded that:

> Students may be well placed to identify both poor practice and potential abuse within settings and college can play an important role in supporting them to make their concerns known, recording them appropriately and following up referrals to children's services.
>
> (Birmingham LSCB, 2013, p 54)

Critical questions

Read the report of the Little Stars SCR and consider the following:

» *How do you think the students used their intuition to analyse the situation at Little Stars?*

» *How were the students supported by their tutors?*

» *How do the lessons from this SCR help you to develop your ability to safeguard children?*

Case study of Little Teds Nursery

In 2009, Vanessa George was arrested following her abuse of children at her nursery. It is important to note that prior to her arrest, the setting had been judged by Ofsted to be satisfactory or good. Although, it was reported that Plymouth's Early Years Advisory Service had regular contact with Little Teds and there had been '*concerns about management and the nursery's ability to adapt to the practices expected. None of these issues raised related to safeguarding*' (Plymouth Safeguarding Children Board, no date).

George had become involved with a man via the internet and it is thought that she then became sexually interested in children. George started to display sexualised behaviour, which included explicit sexual references about adults, to the extent that it became the norm. The abuse carried out by George involved the use of mobile phones. The SCR stated, in the lessons learnt from the report, that:

> Whilst stopping staff carrying mobile phones is an important preventative measure and will mean that images cannot easily be transmitted electronically; this alone will not prevent abuse taking place.
>
> (6.4)

The report concluded that there were several factors that came together which supported a culture where George's sexual abuse was allowed to continue. The factors included:

- absence of a meaningful safeguarding policy in Little Teds;

- lack of awareness by the staff of the inappropriateness of George's increasing sexualised behaviour;

- a lack of formal and rigorous recruitment procedures for staff that meant the recruitment of unsuitable people could be more likely;

- poor management and a lack of accountability.

Critical questions

» *How can these factors contribute to supporting a culture where sexual abuse can continue?*

» *How can the effects of these factors be minimised to help to safeguard children?*

» *What do you think are some of the possible reasons for Ofsted and support services such as the Early Years Advisory Service not picking up on the culture that supported the sexual abuse?*

MANAGER'S VOICE

Putting the theory of safeguarding into practice

Jacky is the manager of an early years setting and below is an extract about safeguarding from the letter she gives to students at the start of their professional practice.

Dear Student

We are committed to keeping all the children in our care safe and we all have a responsibility to report any concerns about another staff member's handling of children or aggressive verbal communication (however minor it appears).

If you have any concerns or worries during your placement please speak immediately to your mentor or to any member of the management team. Jacky is the Designated Safeguarding Offficer (DSO) and Charlotte is the deputy DSO. The yellow folder 'Safeguarding and child protection guidance for Early Years and childcare providers' is kept on the shelf in the office. It provides all the current legislative information and advice as well as contacts for the Local Safeguarding Children Board (LSCB).

Social networking

Please ensure you read our policy on using social network sites during your placement. Under no circumstances should you discuss children or mention where you are on placement or make any other comments that could be misconstrued.

Phones and cameras

Please keep your phone in the hanging pockets in the staffroom. The mobile phone policy is displayed in the staffroom and should be read on your first day. Please only use the nursery camera to take photographs of your activity and print photographs at nursery. Written permission must be obtained from parents if you wish to use any photographs as evidence for your work.

I hope that you find this information useful and that it will help you to fulfil your role as a student in safeguarding the children in our setting.

Best wishes

Jacky

Critical questions

» How do you think Jacky's guidance helps students to identify their safeguarding responsibilities?

» How does the content and approach to safeguarding and child protection differ from the case studies of Little Teds and Little Stars?

» Consider which of Jacky's guidance points relate to safeguarding and which to child protection.

Responsibilities of students

The findings from these SCRs highlight some of the responsibilities you have as a student to contribute to safeguarding children.

Being a suitable person

Part of your responsibility in safeguarding children is being a suitable person to do so, as outlined in the EYFS (DfE, 2014). To be classed as suitable you must not have any serious criminal convictions. All education providers are required to ensure that students complete an application to the Disclosure and Barring Service. At the time of completing the application, it is important that you declare any incident that may have resulted in you having a police record, even if it is not connected with an offence against children. This is because the enhanced search will reveal all incidents and it is better to be honest about any past misdemeanours you may have been involved with. Being honest can be linked to being an ethical practitioner, which is another important facet of you being suitable to work with children and families, particularly in the sensitive area of safeguarding and protection.

Knowledge of factors that can influence safeguarding

Another of your responsibilities is to have knowledge of the children you work with in professional practice. A vital tool here is the use of observations (see Chapter 8). In addition, developing effective ways of working with parents (see Chapter 11) can help you to understand signs of change in children that may indicate there are causes for concern about their safety. As a student, you may have limited contact with parents, therefore you may feel that your contribution has less importance. However, your unique perspective during professional placement can be a useful addition to other information in helping to build up a picture of issues relating to safeguarding, as highlighted in the Little Stars serious case review.

The UK is home to many people from diverse backgrounds and it is important to be aware that many people will be influenced by factors such as culture, colour and religion. Such influences can mean that events can be misinterpreted or misunderstood. The case of Victoria Climbié illustrates the need for practitioners working to safeguard children to be able to think clearly about racism and have knowledge of cultural influences that may be harmful to children or, in Victoria's case, fatal.

CASE STUDY

Victoria Climbié

In 2000, eight year-old Victoria was tortured and murdered by her great-aunt. She had been sent from her home in the African country of the Ivory Coast by her parents to live with her great-aunt so that Victoria could have an education in England. Her death led to an overhaul of child protection policies in the UK.

Lord Laming's Inquiry (DfE, 2003) revealed that part of the reason that action was not taken by the professionals involved in Victoria's case was because she and many of the professionals involved in her case were black. The inquiry heard that non-black people were concerned about the possibility of being accused of being racist and this led to inaction.

Another factor that played a part in Victoria's death was her great-aunt's belief that Victoria was possessed by evil spirits. Victoria's great-aunt was also from the Ivory Coast. Tedam (2014) highlights the abuse of children who are branded as witches capable of harming others and suggests that this '*is a widespread practice in some countries in Africa and across the world*' (p 1). She warns that this is a growing practice in African communities in the UK. A child with disabilities, or who has a condition such as epilepsy, is '*more likely to be called a witch*' (p 4).

Critical questions

»   *What are the cultural and race influences that need to be considered in order to be able to safeguard children effectively?*

»   *What knowledge do you need to have in order to be able to safeguard children from ethnic minorities?*

Chapter reflections

This chapter has summarised your responsibilities as a student in practice in safeguarding children. Part of your responsibility is to have a wide knowledge of and comply with safeguarding policies. Other knowledge includes having an awareness of the differences that can affect children and families that may be a challenge to safeguarding.

Further reading

Department for Education (2011) *The Munro Review of Child Protection: Final Report.* [online] Available at: https://www.gov.uk/government/uploads/system/uploads/attachment_data/file/175391/Munro-Review.pdf (accessed 1 December 2014).

References

Birmingham Safeguarding Children Board (2013) *Serious Case Review.* [online] Available at: www.lscb-birmingham.org.uk/images/stories/downloads/executive-summaries/Published_Overview_Report.pdf (accessed 1 December 2014).

Department for Education (2003) *The Victoria Climbié Inquiry: Report of an inquiry by Lord Laming.* [online] Available at: www.education.gov.uk/publications/eOrderingDownload/CM-5730PDF.pdf (accessed 1 December 2014).

Department for Education (2014) *Statutory Framework for the Early Years Foundation Stage.* London: Crown Copyright. [online] Available at: https://www.gov.uk/government/uploads/system/uploads/attachment_data/file/335504/EYFS_framework_from_1_September_2014__with_clarification_note.pdf (accessed 1 December 2014).

Her Majesty's Government (2013) *Working Together to Safeguard Children: A guide to inter-agency working to safeguard and promote the welfare of children.* [online] Available at: https://www.gov.uk/government/uploads/system/uploads/attachment_data/file/281368/Working_together_to_safeguard_children.pdf (accessed 1 December 2014).

Munro, E (2008) *Effective Child Protection* (2nd edition). London: Sage.

Plymouth Safeguarding Children Board (no date) Serious Case Review into Abuse at Little Teds. [online] Available at: www.plymouth.gov.uk/homepage/.../littletednurseryreview.htm (accessed 1 December 2014).

Tedam, P (2014) Witchcraft Branding and the Abuse of African Children in the UK: Causes, effects and professional interventions. *Early Child Development and Care.* Published online on 24 April, 2014. Available at: dx.doi.org/10.1080/03004430.2014.901015 (accessed 1 December 2014).

5 Key documents

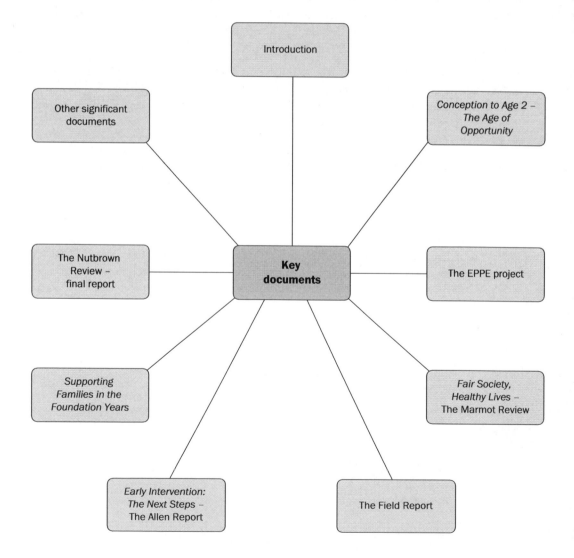

Teachers' Standards (Early Years)

The content of this chapter links to the following Early Years Teacher Award indicators:

1.1, 1.2, 1.3, 2.1, 2.2, 2.3, 2.4, 2.5, 2.6, 2.7, 3.1, 3.2, 3.3, 3.4, 3.5, 4.1, 4.3, 4.4, 5.1, 5.2, 5.3, 5.4, 5.5, 6.1, 6.2, 6.3, 8.1, 8.2, 8.3, 8.4 and 8.7.

Introduction

In this chapter you will find summaries of some key documents that relate to your practice. Having a working knowledge of these documents will also be beneficial when writing assignments as you will invariably be able to fit the context of your assessment to some element of these documents. Reflecting on these reports overall, you will see the government's rationale for its stance on positions such as the school readiness agenda and the introduction of the roles of Early Years Teacher and Early Years Educator.

This chapter cannot do complete justice to the detail that is contained within these key documents and if at all possible you should try to read the original text.

The core curriculum document you will refer to throughout your placement will depend on where you live:

*   England – *Early Years Foundations Stage Statutory Guidance* (2014);
*   Scotland – *Pre-Birth to Three* (2010) and the *Curriculum for Excellence* (2009);
*   *Wales Foundation Phase* (2008);
*   *Northern Ireland Curriculum Guidance for Pre-School Education* (2006).

These documents are not part of this chapter due to word restrictions but familiarity with the one that is relevant to you is essential for a successful placement.

The EPPE project

The Effective Provision of Pre-School Education (EPPE) project was the first longitudinal study in Europe with the aim of determining the impact of pre-school education on children aged three and four years. Begun in 1997, the first results were published in 2002.

Table 5.1 The EPPE project

Main points of the report	What does this mean for your practice?
The study concluded that characteristics of effective learning are found in early years settings that:	• Be assured that what you do can have long-term positive impacts on children and that the qualifications you are pursuing are valuable.

Main points of the report	What does this mean for your practice?
• provide children with a mixture of practitioner-initiated group work and learning through freely chosen play; • provide adult–child interactions that involve 'sustained shared thinking' and open-ended questioning to extend children's thinking; • have practitioners with good curriculum knowledge combined with awareness and understanding of how young children learn; • ensure behaviour policies whereby staff support children in rationalising and talking through their conflicts; • have strong parental involvement, especially in terms of shared educational aims with parents. EPPE also provided evidence regarding the influence of home background on children's outcomes. Children of parents who read to them, took them to the library and sang nursery rhymes with them were better prepared for learning at school, regardless of the parents' educational background, income or social status: *'what parents do with their children is more important than who parents are'* (Sylva et al, 2004, p 5). • The fourth report published in September 2014 found that attending a high quality pre-school had a lasting impact on attainment; the equivalent of achieving eight GCSEs at grade B as opposed to eight GCSEs at grade C (for non-pre-school attendance). In financial terms, the report calculated that *'Attending pre-school was associated with an estimated benefit of around £26,000 per individual'* (Sylva et al, 2014, p 19).	• Children learn best when there is a balance of adult- and child-led activities; this should provide a framework for your planning (see Chapter 8 for further information about planning). • It should inform how you manage children's behaviour. • It should influence how you work with parents; for example, encouraging them to take part in educational trips, and 'stay and play' sessions where you can model how to extend learning and engage children in sustained shared thinking (see Chapter 8 for further information about sustained shared thinking and Chapter 11 for further information about working with parents).

Critical questions

»   *Why is this project important to those working in early years?*

»   *The authors of the report used the ECERS (Early Childhood Environmental Rating Scale) as a standardised way of measuring a quality setting. How would you define quality?*

»   *Whose voice is important in determining quality?*

»   *How would you measure quality in a meaningful way? Is there an alternative?*

Fair Society, Healthy Lives – The Marmot Review

Professor Sir Michael Marmot (2008) chaired this independent review recommending the most effective evidence-based strategies for reducing health inequalities in England from 2010.

Table 5.2 The Marmot Review

Main points of the review	What does this mean for your practice?
• This was the first public health review to emphasise the link between health, poverty and unemployment; that good health was more than the absence of disease (WHO, 1948). • Health inequalities begin in early childhood (starting from the womb) and although later interventions are important, the interventions are considerably less effective where strong early foundations are minimal. • The importance of families in influencing children's educational attainment as opposed to schools was acknowledged, and the review called for closer links between communities, schools and families. • A statistic often referred to from the review is that children who have low cognitive scores at 22 months, but come from affluent home backgrounds, improve their relative scores by the time they reach the age of ten years, while those who have high cognitive scores at 22 months, but come from low socio-economic backgrounds, have diminishing scores as they approach their tenth birthday (p 16). The review's recommendations were aimed at reversing this trend. • The review stressed the importance of children's *readiness for school* (p 18), and of the teaching of skills to increase the chance of success in employment and in life.	• You should set goals that stretch and challenge children of all backgrounds and aim to raise their expectations. • Children who function well in society understand the social conventions that enable people to move easily between social groups, so you should model good manners and a love of learning. • Relationships you form with parents should be respectful and focus on improving outcomes for children. • You should be aware of how children who make the transition from the early years setting to school will progress – for example, techniques used to teach reading and mathematical development – and be committed to your role in laying successful foundations for success.

The Field Report

Frank Field MP (2010) was commissioned to undertake an independent review of poverty and life chances – *The Foundation Years: Preventing poor children becoming poor adults. The report of the Independent Review on Poverty and Life Chances*. One of the review's objectives was to determine the effect of children's home background on their chances of being ready to take advantage of schooling (the implication here is one of 'school readiness', but the actual term was not used then). Throughout the country at the time of the review there was concern about increasing crime, teenage pregnancy, a benefits culture, youth unemployment, low aspirations, drug dependency and a growing divide between middle-class and disadvantaged children. Tackling these problems through intervention in the early years is often referred to as social policy or political drivers.

Table 5.3 The Field Report

Main points of the review	What does this mean for your practice?
• In exploring poverty, the authors found that they were asking the question *'How can we prevent poor children from becoming poor adults?'* and concluded that there needed to be a fundamental change in the way that poverty was tackled other than through income distribution, for example, tax credits. • There was *'overwhelming evidence'* (p 7) that the first five years of a child's life were indicative of their life chances. • For children, what was more important to their future success than money was parental background and education. Good parenting involving opportunities for learning and development, a healthy pregnancy and good maternal health were key. • The importance of attachment and an authoritative parenting style were implied by the use of phrases such as *'secure bonding with the child'* and *'love and responsiveness of parents along with clear boundaries'* (p 7). • Drawing on evidence of brain development in babies the review noted that 80% of a child's brain was formed by the time they reached the age of three. The conclusion was that to make a difference the impact had to be felt within the first three years of a child's life. • The report recommended that investment should be made in *'foundation years'* (p 8) with spending targeted towards developing children's capabilities through expansion of high quality integrated services to both support parents and the capabilities of the poorest children.	• You should model an authoritative style of behaviour management. • You should have high expectations of children regardless of their social background. • Although you may not work with new parents directly, you should encourage new mothers to breastfeed, if they need to, in the setting, perhaps by offering an appropriate chair or just an encouraging smile. • Good mental health of parents impacts on children, so provide opportunities for them to forge supportive friendships with other parents. • Take every opportunity to model how to extend children's learning; for example, by encouraging parents to talk and read to their babies to ensure the basis of sound language development is begun. • Collaborative working with parents and other professionals should be a priority.

Critical questions

» *How can/do practitioners raise children's expectations and aspirations?*

» *What are the implications of this if children's biggest influence is from the home?*

Early Intervention: The next steps – **The Allen Report**

The MP Graham Allen was commissioned by the government to write this report to assess how children from disadvantaged backgrounds could be given the best start in life; the results were published in 2011. It drew on reports from Ofsted inspectors that some children were beginning school unable to speak in sentences or recognise the difference between numbers and letters.

Table 5.4 The Allen Report

Main points of the report	What does this mean for your practice?
• The report spoke of the importance of children being '*school ready*' (p 53). • Substantiated by evidence from the OECD (Organisation for Economic Co-operation and Development) the report argued the economic case for intervening early in children's lives. • Based on evidence from previous reports in this country and internationally, as well as growing research regarding the development of the human brain, the report made recommendations that parents should be given support to create for their children a home environment essential for school success. • Parenting programmes such as Triple P were advocated, as well as regular assessment of children's development.	• You should have a critical understanding of how to prepare children to take advantage of opportunities at school. • As you interact more with parents an understanding of parenting programmes and a parent's readiness for change will enable you to suggest enrolment in the best parenting course for families.

Supporting Families in the Foundation Years

The *Supporting Families* document (DfE, 2011) was jointly published by the Department for Education and the Department of Health and was the government's official response to previously commissioned reviews. It agreed with the Field Report (2010) that investment in the foundation years with support for parents and families is the most cost-effective way of breaking the cycle of inter-generational child poverty and enabling social mobility. The moral and economic argument for doing this was explained, together with recommendations for how this could be done.

Table 5.5 Supporting Families in the Foundation Years

Main points of the report	What does this mean for your practice?
• The report stated that a key aim for children's development should be 'school readiness' which it defined as: 'Learning to walk and run, to speak and communicate, to relate to others, to play, explore their own curiosity, and to enjoy learning through their play, as well as beginning to read and write and use numbers' (p 18). • Parenting skills and advice and support for parents were identified as key priorities – particularly the need to engage fathers in the lives of their children. • It also emphasised the need to encourage men into Foundation Stage professions. • The importance of a well qualified and motivated workforce was reiterated and the government committed itself to having a graduate-led early years workforce.	• You should be aware of all the factors necessary for school success and support children as they make the transition to school. • You should make an effort to involve fathers; for example, some fathers may feel uncomfortable in a predominantly female environment and you should take steps to try to overcome this. • Build trusting and productive relationships with parents, knowing where to signpost them to relevant services to improve their situation as necessary.

Critical questions

» The authors of this report state that 'the moral argument' for intervention is clear (p 8). What do you think they mean by this?

» Why do you think it is important for them to stress the moral argument as well as the economic case?

» Do you agree that having more men working in early years professions is important? Give reasons for your answer.

The Nutbrown Review – final report

In 2012, Professor Cathy Nutbrown accepted an invitation from the Minister for Children and Families to lead the review of early education and childcare qualifications. The final report was called *Foundations for Quality* but is most commonly referred to as The Nutbrown Review.

Table 5.6 The Nutbrown Review

Main points of the review	What does this mean for your practice?
• The review recognised the high-quality practice evidenced by many in the childcare profession, but raised concern about the lack of trust shown by some employers towards the consistency of some early years qualifications.	• Ensure that you understand the significance of secure attachments for children and demonstrate this through spending time interacting with babies and children, showing genuine interest in their worries and joys.
• It called for those working with babies and young children to provide love and warmth and to have an understanding of child development, play and the way children learn and to know how this could be effectively implemented.	• You should have a good knowledge of child development and know how to extend learning by being aware of the next steps for each child's progress.
• The review recommended that the sector become more professional with clear career pathways and roles.	• Although the status of early years is not where many would like it to be yet, it has come a long way in the last 20 years. You should be prepared to be an ambassador for graduate-led provision by not becoming complacent but genuinely aiming to make a difference to children's development.
• Early years specialist graduates should achieve Qualified Teacher Status (QTS) because it was acknowledged that highly qualified staff are more effective in supporting children's language and communication, reasoning, thinking and mathematical skill (for further information on the professionalism of the workforce see Chapter 3).	
• There were clear implications for students, with the recommendation that they experience practice in a variety of settings (at least three) that had an Ofsted rating of 'Good' or 'Outstanding'.	• You should encourage others to continue their professional development by being enthusiastic about how your own training has benefitted you.
	• You should only choose placements with an Ofsted rating of 'Good' or 'Outstanding' and should select different practice placements to ensure that you are gaining breadth and depth of experience.
• It was also recommended that practitioners work sensitively with parents, as they were the greatest influence on children's *values, behaviours and ambitions*' (p 11).	• Take every opportunity to work with parents and be involved in multi-agency working.
• It stressed the importance of collaboration with other professionals so that individual children's needs are identified and met.	• While in practice you should reflect on your own commitment to being a pedagogical leader.
• The review also called for pedagogical leadership from all practitioners: '*Ultimately, all Early Years practitioners should aspire to be leaders, of practice, if not of settings, and all practitioners should be capable of demonstrating some pedagogical leadership regardless of qualification level*' (p 55).	

Critical questions

» What are the key differences between 'Satisfactory', 'Good' and 'Outstanding' settings? Can you think of arguments for and against students being allowed to attend placements in 'Satisfactory' settings? (NB The 'Satisfactory' outcome is no longer applicable as an Ofsted award. It was replaced by 'Requires improvement' in 2012).

» What are the similarities and differences between being a leader and a pedagogical leader? Make a comparative list.

» How realistic is it to expect all in early years settings to be pedagogical leaders? Why do you think this?

Conception to Age 2 – The Age of Opportunity

This report (Wave Trust and DfE, 2013) was the Department for Education's response to *Supporting Families in the Foundation Years*.

Table 5.7 Conception to Age 2 – The Age of Opportunity

Main points of the report	What does this mean for your practice?
• There was an acknowledgement that, for policy makers, the early years had once begun at the age of eight, then five and then three. However, in light of compelling evidence from a growing understanding of brain development, there was new recognition that the first 1001 days of a child's life – from the womb to two – was the most crucial time to make a positive, enduring impact upon children's well-being and prospective outcomes.	• Many students avoid the baby room; however, given the critical importance of the first two years of life this is somewhere where you, as a higher level practitioner, should aim to spend time gaining knowledge and understanding of child development and attachment.
• Many of the costly and troubling ills in society (for example, substance abuse, domestic violence, poor physical and mental health, unemployment) were neither inevitable nor unmanageable.	• If you have the opportunity, consider asking the setting leader if you can become a shadow key person for a baby, making notes on development and interacting with parents. This will give you valuable experience that you can draw upon when you are a professional practitioner.
• Public services had traditionally been reactive rather than preventative; an estimated 40% of public funds were spent on problems that could have been anticipated and prevented if support had been given during those crucial first 1001 days.	• You should also take the opportunity to develop your emotional intelligence by choosing to act rather than react in difficult circumstances. Maintaining a calm and positive attitude not only creates a better working atmosphere for staff, but is also better for vulnerable and impressionable babies.
• In economic terms the report calculated that for every £1 invested there was a return of between £1.37 and £9.20 (p 5).	• If possible, work with other agencies involved with individual children. This will give you some idea of the drivers and barriers in collaborative working.

Main points of the report	What does this mean for your practice?
• Much of this report reiterated the case for early intervention. However, what was new was the emphasis given to relationships.	
• Firstly, the significance of secure connections between parents and children to prevent insecure/disorganised attachment was recognised as being vital, and also connections between children and practitioners were key for good mental health in the future (35–40% of parental–infant attachments were estimated to be insecure/disorganised, p 17).	
• Secondly, in order to achieve this, everyone in the early years workforce needed a good knowledge of holistic child development, along with the skills to build and sustain trusting relationships. Of '*fundamental importance*' was the '*emotional intelligence (or competence) of the Early Years' sector workforce*' (p 35).	
• Thirdly, to be efficient and effective, good relationships leading to the integration of multi-agency services for children were seen as crucial.	
• Supervision by an experienced mentor was also stated as being '*not an option*' but a necessity (p 96).	

Critical questions

» *Is it possible to be sure what the savings from intervention might be? Why do you think this?*

» *Do you think it is reasonable for practitioners to be expected to be responsible for solving problems in society associated with poverty and disadvantage?*

Other significant documents

The previous section outlined reports and research that have shaped the position of recent government policy and initiatives. This section briefly summarises other significant documents that have influenced early years policy and practice in the past, which have relatively few recommendations related to early years settings but are still influential in important ways (for example, The Munro Review (2011)). The main elements of some of these documents can be seen to underpin the reports outlined above (eg the UNCRC), while others (*Every Child Matters*) are no longer part of government policy.

United Nations Convention on the Rights of the Child (UNCRC)

The 1989 convention was significant because for the first time childhood was recognised as a unique phase rather than a preparation for adulthood (Tomlinson, 2013). Having ratified the convention in 1991 the government in the UK is obliged to consider the best interests of the child when creating policy. The 54 articles in the convention address diverse rights, including protection and safety. Below are listed the rights most likely to impact on your practice. Children have the right to:

- non-discrimination (Article 2);

- have their needs taken as the primary concern in decisions that affect them (Article 3);

- parental guidance (Article 5);

- be listened to (Article 12);

- special care if they are disabled (Article 23);

- education (Article 29);

- play and relax (Article 31).

Critical questions

»   *What are the implications of these rights for your practice?*

»   *Given that children have a right to a voice in decisions that affect them, if a child refuses to have their nappy changed should you insist?*

Every Child Matters

The Green Paper *Every Child Matters* (DfES, 2003) was seen as a response to the death of Victoria Climbié and formed the underpinning philosophy of childcare services in the ten years following its publication. Its five key principles advocated that children should be healthy, safe, enjoy and achieve, make a positive contribution and achieve economic well-being.

The Munro Review

The introduction of the Children Act 1989 marked the beginning of a shift in thinking regarding promoting good outcomes for children. There was a growing acceptance that it was everyone's responsibility to promote the welfare of children; the focus changed from child protection, which was more reactionary and generally involved action after an episode of abuse had occurred, to safeguarding children (Children Act, 2004) which was more preventative (see Chapter 4 for more information on safeguarding).

As with the reviews led by Frank Field MP (2010), Graham Allen MP (2011) and Dame Clare Tickell (2011), The Munro Review drew on the growing body of evidence of the effectiveness of early intervention, surmising that preventative rather than reactive services are more effective in reducing abuse and neglect.

Critical question

» *Make a comparative table of new and previously conveyed findings from the reports and reviews in the chapter. What do you notice?*

STUDENT VOICE

Natalie

As a student I always found government documents difficult to understand and one of the challenges I faced was being able to break the information down in order to find the relevant parts for my work.

To overcome this I would create a table of key points for myself and work through different sections of the document, highlighting important and useful words or phrases that I thought would give me the depth I needed to enhance my assignments.

Chapter reflections

This chapter has introduced highly influential documents from the past 20 years that have influenced national early years policy, local authority policy, your placement policies and, therefore, your practice. Reflecting on the evidence underpinning these documents will give you a critical understanding of why there is emphasis on certain practices as well as the confidence to argue the case for early years investment and training based on an understanding of the evidence. It should also make you reflect on the important role that you will undertake in improving the lives of children and families.

Further reading

Baldock, P, Fitzgerald, D and Kay, J (2013) *Understanding Early Years Policy* (3rd edition). London: Sage.

Tomlinson, P (2013) *Early Years Policy and Practice: A critical alliance*. Northwich: Critical Publishing.

References

Allen, G (2011) *Early Intervention: The next steps.* [online] Available at: https://www.gov.uk/government/uploads/system/uploads/attachment_data/file/284086/early-intervention-next-steps2.pdf (accessed 1 December 2014).

Department for Children, Education, Lifelong Learning and Skills, (2008) *Foundation Phase Framework for Children's Learning for 3–7-year-olds in Wales.* [online] Available at: www.wales.gov.uk/dcells/publications/policy_strategy_and_planning/early-wales/whatisfoundation/foundation-phase/2274085/frameworkforchildrene.pdf?lang=en (accessed 1 December 2014).

Department for Education (2011) *Supporting Families in the Foundation Years*. [online] Available at: https://www.gov.uk/government/uploads/system/uploads/attachment_data/file/184868/DFE-01001-2011_supporting_families_in_the_foundation_years.pdf (accessed 1 December 2014).

Department for Education (2014) *Statutory Framework for the Early Years Foundation Stage*. London: Crown Copyright. [online] Available at: https://www.gov.uk/government/uploads/system/uploads/attachment_data/file/335504/EYFS_framework_from_1_September_2014__with_clarification_note.pdf (accessed 1 December 2014).

Department of Education, Department of Health, Social Services and Public Safety (2006) *Curriculum Guidance for Pre-School Education*. [online] Available at: www.deni.gov.uk/index/support-and-development-2/early-years-education/16-pre-school-education-curricularguidance-pg.htm (accessed 1 December 2014).

Department for Education and Skills (2003) *Every Child Matters* (Green Paper). London: HMSO. [online] Available at: webarchive.nationalarchives.gov.uk/20130401151715/http://www.education.gov.uk/publications/eOrderingDownload/CM5860.pdf (accessed 1 December 2014).

Fact Sheet: A summary of rights under the Convention of the Rights of the Child (no date) [online] Available at: www.unicef.org/crc/files/Rights_overview.pdf (accessed 1 December 2014).

Field, F (2010) *The Foundation Years: Preventing poor children becoming poor adults. The report of the Independent Review on Poverty and Life Chances*. London: Crown Copyright. [online] Available at: dera.ioe.ac.uk/14156/1/poverty-report.pdf (accessed 1 December 2014).

Learning and Teaching Scotland (2010) *Pre-Birth to Three: Positive Outcomes for Scotland's Children and Families*. [online] Available at: www.educationscotland.gov.uk/Images/PreBirthToThreeBooklet_tcm4-633448.pdf (accessed 1 December 2014).

Marmot, M. (2010) *Fair Society, Healthy Lives*. [online] Available at: www.instituteofhealthequity.org/projects/fair-society-healthy-lives-the-marmot-review (accessed 1 December 2014).

Munro, E (2011) *The Munro Review of Child Protection Final Report: The child's journey*. London: DfE. [online] Available at: https://www.gov.uk/government/uploads/system/uploads/attachment_data/file/175391/Munro-Review.pdf (accessed 1 December 2014).

Nutbrown, C (2012) *Foundations for Quality. The independent review of early education and childcare qualifications. Final Report*. Runcorn: Crown Copyright. [online] Available at: https://www.gov.uk/government/uploads/system/uploads/attachment_data/file/175463/Nutbrown-Review.pdf (accessed 1 December 2014).

Scottish Government (2009) *Curriculum for Excellence*. [online] Available at: www.educationscotland.gov.uk/Images/all_experiences_outcomes_tcm4-539562.pdf (accessed 1 December 2014).

Sylva, K, Melhuish, E, Sammons, P, Siraj-Blatchford, I and Taggart, B (2004) *The Effective Provision of Pre-School Education (EPPE) Project: Findings from Pre-School to end of Key Stage 1*. [online] Available at: www.ioe.ac.uk/RB_Final_Report_3-7.pdf (accessed 1 December 2014).

Sylva, K, Melhuish, E, Sammons, P, Siraj, I, Taggart, B, Smees, R, Toth, K, Welcomme, W and Hollingworth, K (2014) *Students' Educational and Developmental Outcomes at Age 16. Effective Pre-school, Primary and Secondary Education (EPPSE 3–16) Project. Research Report*. [online] Available at: https://www.gov.uk/government/uploads/system/uploads/attachment_data/file/351496/RR354_-_Students__educational_and_developmental_outcomes_at_age_16.pdf (accessed 1 December 2014).

The Children Act 2004 (c.31) London: HMSO. [online] Available at: www.legislation.gov.uk/ukpga/2004/31/pdfs/ukpga_20040031_en.pdf (accessed 1 December 2014).

Tickell, Dame C (2011) *The Early Years: Foundations for life, health and learning – an independent report on the early years foundation stage to Her Majesty's Government.* London: Crown Copyright. [online] Available at: https://www.gov.uk/government/uploads/system/uploads/attachment_data/file/180919/DFE-00177-2011.pdf (accessed 1 December 2014).

Tomlinson, P (2013) *Early Years Policy and Practice: A critical alliance.* Northwich: Critical Publishing.

Wave Trust *Tackling the Roots of Disadvantage* – in collaboration with the Department for Education (2013) *Conception to Age 2: The age of opportunity. Addendum to the Government's Vision for the Foundation Years: 'Supporting Families in the Foundation Years'.* [online] Available at: www.wavetrust.org/sites/default/files/reports/conception-to-age-2-full-report_0.pdf (accessed 1 December 2014).

World Health Organisation definition of health (1948) [online] Available at: www.who.int/about/definition/en/print.html (accessed 1 December 2014).

6 Your first day

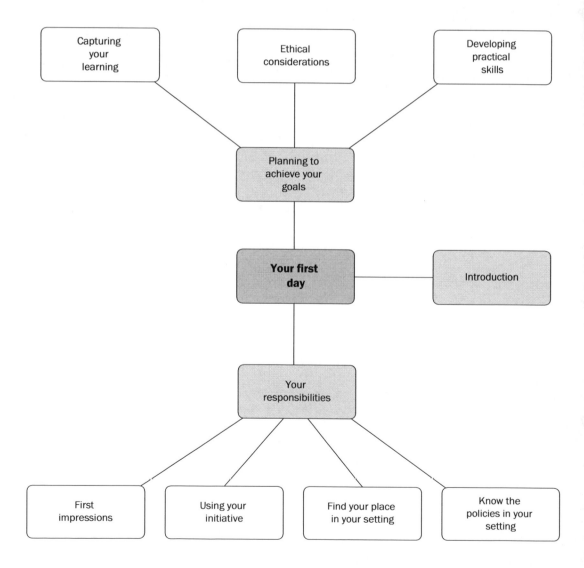

Teachers' Standards (Early Years)

The content of this chapter links to the following Early Years Teacher Award indicators:

8.1, 8.2, 8.3, 8.4 and 8.6.

Introduction

This chapter helps you to plan for and manage your first day in your new setting. Chapter 2 explained the importance of preparing carefully for your placement. Please read the information in that chapter in conjunction with this one. Hopefully, by the time your first day arrives, you should feel well prepared and have an understanding of what to expect and any problems will have been sorted out. Your first day is incredibly important in shaping your professional placement experience and this chapter gives you some points to consider in order to help you make the whole of your placement a great success.

Your responsibilities

As a student, you are in the position of being a privileged guest in your setting. This position brings many responsibilities for you to consider and there is an expectation that you behave professionally at all times. Chapter 3 discusses the concept of professionalism in more detail and explores the theories that underpin definitions of professionalism. This chapter looks at some of the practical aspects of how you can convey your professionalism in your placement from day one. It also outlines some of your responsibilities as a student.

First impressions

It is your responsibility to do as much as you can to make a positive first impression. A very simple way of creating a good impression is to show that you are a friendly person by smiling and saying hello and, where appropriate, introducing yourself by your first name. The practitioners will be keen to get to know you as well. Below Jacky describes how she welcomes students to her setting and she has written about the strategies she uses to get to know them.

MANAGER'S VOICE

Welcome!

Dear Student

Welcome to our setting, we hope you will find it a valuable learning experience.

We believe in providing a loving and caring environment for the children in our care and we encourage the children and staff to care for and support each other. Children learn through their social experiences and they will observe and learn from you as much as you observe and learn from them.

In order for us to support you and your individual needs and learning styles we need to get to know you, therefore we would be pleased if you could tell us a bit about yourself. You could do this by talking to all the staff and children – as you work with us, talk to us about your course, your needs, your strengths and the areas you would like to develop. In turn, practice your communication and collaboration skills by finding out about the staff team, our qualifications, our pedagogies and our own learning journeys.

Best wishes

Jacky

Practitioners value students' abilities to interact with children very highly; it is something that they almost always comment on when giving feedback about students. Therefore, ensure that you take the opportunity to interact with children in appropriate ways right from the start. The importance of relationships and suggestions about interacting with children are discussed in Chapter 12.

Appearing confident can give a good first impression. Although it can be difficult to appear confident if you are nervous about being in your new environment, taking the initiative in introducing yourself in a friendly way can help to break the ice. It can also be tricky to get the right balance between appearing self-assured and overly confident. However, knowledge about your setting will help you to gain confidence, so ensure that you increase your knowledge by finding out about the policies and routines of your setting.

Know the policies in your setting

It is the responsibility of your mentor to ensure that you are made aware of the setting's policies and it is likely that they will be pointed out to you as part of your induction. It is your responsibility to ensure that you read the policies carefully and understand the procedures to follow. In particular, it is important that you are aware of the policies relating to:

- safeguarding and whistleblowing: see Chapter 4 for more details;

- health and safety: eg ensure you are aware of children with medical needs and are able to identify children with allergies;

- first aid procedure: ensure you know what to do in the event of a child becoming unwell or sustaining an injury;

- behaviour policy.

Find your place in your setting

Finding out how the staff in your setting view students will help you to fit in right from the start. Ask if there are any rules that you should be aware of. For example, some settings welcome students as potentially valued colleagues and happily share the staffroom and resources generously with student colleagues. However, other settings may not be as inclusive and students may be expected to take their breaks separately. Be prepared to make the best of whatever situation you are faced with and remember that as you are a guest in the setting you have to graciously comply with their practices.

Use your initiative

When practitioners are contacted for feedback about students, almost without fail they comment on how well students have used their initiative. The dictionary defines initiative as *'the ability to assess and initiate things independently and the power or opportunity to act or take charge before others do'*. If you use your initiative right from the start of your placement you will help staff form a positive impression of you. You can start to show your initiative by carefully watching and listening to what is going on and by learning the routine of the setting. Examples of routines that you should take note of include:

*   how the setting manages the transition from indoor to outdoor play;

*   procedures for arrival and departure of the children and information sharing with parents;

*   meal and snack times.

Ensuring that you are following their procedures will help you to take the lead in anticipating how you can support the staff and children.

Planning to achieve your goals

You should be allocated a mentor while you are in your placement. The role of your mentor is to support you and help to maximise your learning opportunities. Your mentor will be able to fulfil this objective if you have a clear understanding of the academic work you need to complete and a list of skills that you need to practise. Having a list will mean that your mentor will quickly be able to identify times and opportunities for you to gather evidence for your work. This is especially important if you are on a short placement. You may find the skills and knowledge audit (see Appendix 2) will help you to identify some goals to achieve during your placement.

Developing practical skills

Being in your placement should give you the chance to develop some practical skills that you may not have had the opportunity to develop previously. Therefore, it is helpful to identify some of these skills, as well as concentrating on knowledge and learning theory. Again, the skills and knowledge audit template included in Appendix 2 may be useful here. Jacky makes a point of letting students know how important it is that they share with practitioners exactly what practical experiences they would like to have the opportunity to develop.

MANAGER'S VOICE

Practical skills

Dear Student

Hopefully you will have highlighted any practical skills that you would like to learn or practice in your introductions to the placement. If you don't tell us what it is you are unsure of or worried about we may not be of help to you! We are happy to teach you and let you practice skills such as nappy changing, making up bottles, planning and assessing children (under direct or indirect supervision) etc. We would be pleased to provide you with a certificate of competency in any skill(s) you learn while you are with us if you would like one.

Above all we hope you enjoy your placement. Please let us know as soon as possible if you have any concerns or need any help with your work or assignments.

Jacky

Ethical considerations

It is an ethical responsibility to ensure that you negotiate how and when you are going to achieve your goals with your mentor and all staff in your setting in a collaborative way. Such collaboration should also include the children and parents. Abbie explains how she approached some of the ethical considerations related to conducting her work during her placement:

STUDENT VOICE

Abbie

Dear Student

Going on placement can be a daunting and difficult process, which is why it is important to balance the demands of being a student with the needs of the placement. It is essential to prepare the children for this procedure and ensure that I carry out tasks 'with' the setting not 'on' the setting. I think it is important to inform the staff of the tasks I am hoping to carry out during placement and find out when to do them. When undertaking a task with a child, I would make sure that the child is aware of the procedure that is taking place and explain why I am doing it. I would also work with my mentor to ensure that the parents are happy for me to carry out the tasks with their child. This will guarantee that I am not conducting research for my tasks without the setting's permission and consent.

Abbie

Critical questions

» *How does Abbie's approach help her to work 'with' the setting and not 'on' the setting?*

» *How could her approach help to gain co-operation for completing her tasks in the setting?*

» *What skills and qualities will Abbie be using and developing in adopting an ethical and collaborative approach to her work?*

» *How can you ensure you have the permission of the child to carry out research with them?*

Capturing your learning

It is really important that you take the opportunity to capture and reflect upon the informal and informal aspects of your learning (see Reed and Canning, 2010). It is a good idea to ensure that you are equipped to do this from your very first day. Capturing informal learning can be achieved in the following ways:

• Take photos of your practical work: for example, you may have created a display. As always, bear in mind your ethical responsibilities; for example, do not take photographs of children in your setting, and ensure that you maintain anonymity about anything that you write down. It is important that you do not assume you have permission to take photos, so check the procedure first.

• Make notes in your reflective diary or journal. This is an important way of noting incidents that help your understanding of children's education and care. These notes may be observations of children or examples of constructive feedback from practitioners. Writing down helps you to reflect upon their significance and will contribute to your professional practice. See Chapter 13 for more about reflective practice.

Chapter reflections

This chapter should help you to plan carefully for your first day so that you can get off to a great start and make the most of your placement. By careful planning and following the suggestions above, it is likely that you will have a really useful and enjoyable placement. Occasionally, unexpected situations will arise and if that happens it is really important that you talk to somebody who can support you. The nature of the issue will guide you in making the decision of who to speak to. Hopefully, you will be able to approach your mentor, but sometimes the problem may be something that is difficult to bring up with your mentor. In this situation you should contact the appropriate person in your university. This is likely to be your tutor and they will be able to help you to work out a strategy to manage the issue. It is unlikely that you will be advised to leave a setting, unless there are serious problems such as safeguarding issues. Remember that settings are not obliged to offer you their time and support, so it is up to you to do your utmost to make the most of your placement and aim to make a positive contribution. This will hopefully ensure you have an outstanding experience.

Further reading

Nutbrown, C (2012) *Foundations for Quality. The independent review of early education and childcare qualifications. Final Report.* Runcorn: Crown Copyright. [online] Available at: https://www.gov.uk/government/uploads/system/uploads/attachment_data/file/175463/Nutbrown-Review.pdf (accessed 1 December 2014).

Rose, R and Rogers, S (2012) *The Role of the Adult in Early Years Settings.* Maidenhead: Open University Press.

Reference

Reed, M and Canning, C (2010) *Reflective Practice in the Early Years.* London: Sage.

7 Linking theory to practice

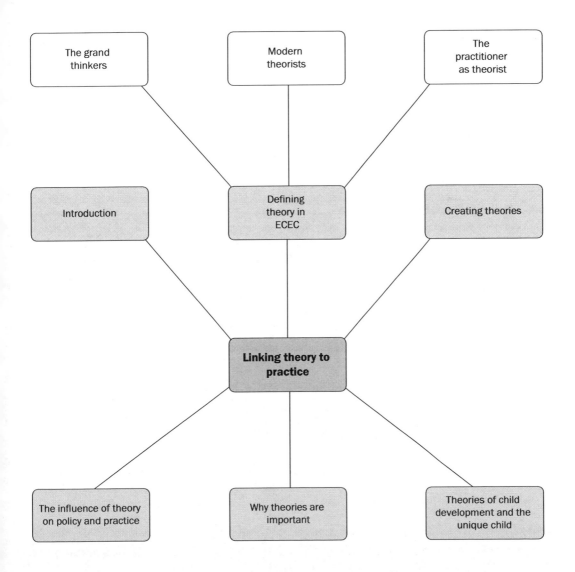

Introduction

Theories of child development have traditionally been part of the content of all or most courses leading to early years qualifications. This chapter explores some of the reasons why it is important to understand the place of theory in Early Childhood Education and Care (ECEC). It highlights the legacy of the '*grand thinkers*' (David et al, 2003), who have informed our understanding of how children learn and develop. It does not explore the content of the theories in detail because this has been achieved elsewhere, for example, Nutbrown et al (2008) and Pound (2005). However, the aim of this chapter is not to simply discuss the theorists from the past, it is to encourage you to explore the theories that underpin the current practices relating to ECEC, and, most importantly, to encourage you to theorise about your own practice. Also included are the thoughts of student practitioners, Emily and Charlotte, who share their ideas about what they have learned about the importance of theory and how it relates to practice. It is important to be aware that one theory cannot be applied to all children and as practitioners it is vital to bear in mind the uniqueness of each child. The chapter concludes with some questions to help you to critically reflect on how theory can enhance your practice and promote the development of the children in your care.

Creating theories

Theories can be informed by research. Such research may be conducted by academics who, after analysing their data, look for meaning in it and then draw conclusions, thus creating a theory. Their findings are disseminated in publications, such as books or journals. For example, some of the research that has been conducted with children has resulted in theories being created about how we think children learn (Figure 7.1). Such findings have informed government policy about early childhood education. One example of a government policy that has been informed by theories of how children learn is England's Early Years Foundation Stage Framework (DfE, 2014).

Figure 7.1 *Creating theories from research about how children learn and develop*

Defining theory in ECEC

A theory can be described as a system of ideas intended to explain why and how something occurs. A theory can also be described as an idea that is used to account for a situation or justify a course of action. In ECEC there are many theories that influence our understanding of how we plan care and education for children. In order to gain an understanding of how theories can influence your practice, this chapter encourages you to think about theorists in the following categories:

- the 'grand thinkers';

- modcrn theorists;

- the practitioner as theorist.

Categories of theorists

The grand thinkers

Much of what we do with, and for, children is informed by the work of theorists, many of whom lived and worked in the first half of the last century. Such theorists are often described as the '*grand thinkers*' (David et al, 2003), because they were the first people whose ideas about human behaviour helped us to gain insight into how children develop. Jean Piaget, for example, fits into this category. He was a psychologist whose work has helped us to understand that children think and learn in ways that are different from adults. To illustrate this point, the first stage of Piaget's theory of cognitive development is the 'sensori-motor' stage. This means that, according to Piaget's theory, children aged 0–2 years learn through their senses and movement. Take a moment to reflect on the sorts of activities for babies and toddlers that you may have seen in your professional practice. As an example, you may have seen babies engaging with a treasure basket containing objects such as lemons and pine cones. As they pick up the objects from the basket, they are developing their fine motor (movement) skills. As they hold them to their mouths, they use their senses to smell and feel the objects. Table 7.1 provides a summary of some of the grand thinkers and their theories.

Table 7.1 The 'grand thinkers' who have influenced ECEC

Name	Dates of birth and death	Country of birth	Legacy to ECEC
Friedrich Froebel	1782–1852	Germany	Introduced the concept of 'kindergarten'. Introduced women into teaching. Emphasised the importance of play and working with parents.

Name	Dates of birth and death	Country of birth	Legacy to ECEC
Sigmund Freud	1856–1939	Czech Republic	Known as the father of psychoanalysis, his work influenced understanding of the importance of play in helping children's social and emotional development.
Jean Piaget	1896–1980	Switzerland	Promoted an understanding that children think differently from adults.
Lev Vygotsky	1896–1934	Russia	Developed the theory of the 'zone of proximal development'.

Highlighted the role of the adult in supporting children's learning. |
| Burrhus Skinner | 1904–1990 | USA | Behaviour management. |
| John Bowlby | 1907–1990 | England | Attachment theory. |
| Jerome Bruner | 1915– | USA | Modes of representation.

The importance of social interactionism. |
| Margaret Donaldson | 1926– | Scotland | Emphasised the importance of focusing on what children can do, rather than what they cannot do.

Identified the importance of child-centred education. |

Other people who could also be regarded as grand thinkers are people who were pioneers of early childhood education and created theories about educational approaches for young children. Such people include Maria Montessori, the McMillan sisters, Rudolf Steiner and Susan Isaacs.

Critical questions

Take some time to find out more about the 'grand thinkers' (see further reading) and then consider the following.

» *What are the main points of their theories?*

» *Can you identify the work of the theorists and pioneers and apply them to activities that you have observed in your professional practice? For example, as discussed above, Piaget theorised that children aged 0–2 years are in the sensori-motor stage of learning. How can you see his theory reflected in planning and play for babies and children?*

» *Reflect on your professional experience working with very young children. Can you identify examples of how theories can explain the planning for children's learning? How is this reflected in babies' and children's play?*

» *Which of the theorists considered above do you think has most relevance to contemporary ECEC and why?*

Modern theorists

The grand thinkers from the past have created a legacy of work that has helped modern-day theorists to continue to develop theories about how children learn and develop. For example, Chris Athey (2007) developed Piaget's schema theory. More recently, Cathy Nutbrown (2012) has explored how children learn by observing other children. The grand thinkers, together with the modern theorists, provide a framework (sometimes referred to as a 'theoretical framework') to help you understand a great deal about how children learn and develop, and this in turn helps you to plan for children's learning.

The practitioner as theorist

So far, this chapter has discussed the place of theorists who have become well known because of the research they have published about children's learning and development. However, it is important for you to realise that as practitioners, you are also theorists. This is because part of your work involves observing the babies and young children in your care. Formal observations are a vital part of understanding children, and this is a reason why they are a statutory requirement in the EYFS (see Chapter 8). Consider that as you observe children, you are being a researcher in the same way as the theorists discussed in the previous sections. You are collecting data in your observations. Careful analysis of what you have seen while observing children will help you to draw your own conclusions about how you can promote children's learning and development. You will be able to compare what you see with what you have learned from the grand thinkers and modern theorists in order to create your own theories.

Why theories are important

A theory helps you to understand why you do what you do. As practitioners working with young children, it is vital that you have an understanding of how children develop and learn. If children are not learning and developing as anticipated, you may need to identify areas of support in order to promote their potential and maximise their development.

Part of our understanding of how children learn can be gained from observing children in their setting. Tina Bruce (2001) explains how theories help us understand what we are seeing when we observe children:

> *Theories help us to predict and to anticipate how children might behave and react. They help us to structure what we observe. Theories help us to make sense of what we see ... when we analyse play, we find ourselves linking what we have found with what other people (theorists) have found. We may find our observations fit with theories. We may find that they do not. This will help us to think deeply.*
>
> (p 19)

Bruce suggests that in order to understand what we are observing, we need to have knowledge about theories as a framework to interrogate what we are seeing. Her words suggest that we do not have to see theories replicated exactly in our observations. As informed practitioners you will use your knowledge of child development to analyse your observations and you will decide how they converge or diverge with theories of child development. Bruce also highlights the importance of deep thinking that is necessary to critically reflect on what you have observed. Thus, in your role as practitioner and as theorist, you will create your own theories about the children you care for and educate. To illustrate this point, read Emily's entry in her professional practice competency file where she explains how her understanding of theories informed her practice.

CASE STUDY

A student's example of how theory can support practice

During my last placement I followed the theory of many early years pioneers by encouraging the children to become involved with free play and also to explore natural resources and nature by playing outside. This was shown when I set up the water play as an activity for the children. This activity allowed the children to freely play with my support to further their development, which is supported by Vygotsky and his zone of proximal development theory as well as Froebel's theory that children develop naturally through play.

Reflection on impact of activity for this competency

Educational theories have helped me to help the children's development, especially by following Vygotsky's views, because all of the settings I have been in allow the children a lot of free play time of which initially I was unsure of the outcome, but as Pound (2005, p 73) states, 'play must be open-ended' and we should allow the children to reach their own goals at their own pace. However, Froebel and Vygotsky share the view that says we should know when to intervene with children's play to allow them to develop further and guide them to reach their full potential. As Pound (2005, p 40) says, the zone of proximal development is not just a 'child's existing knowledge but also their ability to learn with help'. I did this within the water play activity as I sat near to the table and I listened to the children and gave them the time to try and work out any issues and suggested ideas if I saw they needed the support.

Comment on case study

Emily's account shows she has reflected on how her knowledge of theory has supported the decisions she made about her practice. Initially she was unsure about the practice of allowing children to engage in free play, but through her knowledge of theory and her own experiments with it, she was able to know what to do with children, not only because that was what she saw others doing, but also because she knew it would develop children's learning. She was now in a position to justify her practice. Figure 7.2 shows how Emily linked theory to practice. See Chapter 13 for more about reflective practice.

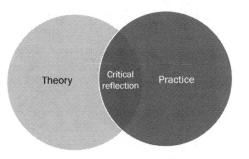

Figure 7.2 *How critical reflection can help link theory to practice*

Theories of child development and the unique child

Although we use theories to help us understand children, as already stated, it must be remembered that each child is unique. This is a paradoxical situation because on the one hand, we say that it is important to observe children (see Chapter 8) in order to plan for their individual needs, while on the other hand, we say that it is important to analyse the observations by drawing on theories of child development that appear to be applicable to all children. It is important to take a critical approach to theories and not accept them as being appropriate for all children. One reason for being critical about the application of a theory for all children is because the majority of the grand thinkers whose theories have influenced early childhood were predominantly European males and much of their research was conducted on participants who were European children. This is an important point to consider because it is now recognised that, as David et al (2003) state, we have become increasingly aware of how theories of child development are not always applicable to non-European children. This is because there are cultural differences in the role of children in society (see below). There are many factors that can affect children's development and it is important that such factors are taken into consideration.

Influences on children's development

- *Context and environment* can mean that a child may behave differently in an unfamiliar environment. For example, young children may find transitions from home to a new setting difficult and they may regress in their development until they become confident and familiar with their new environment.

- *Cultural expectations* of children's role in society can influence adults' expectations of how children behave and develop. Chan (2004) explored the effect of culture on Chinese children living in Hong Kong. As a former British colony, early childhood practices in Hong Kong were heavily influenced by western theories. However, the majority of inhabitants of Hong Kong are Chinese and their theories of children's development have been shaped by thousands of years of Chinese culture. Chan points out that Chinese parents and teachers disregard the contribution that play makes towards a child's development. However, in western theories of child development, play is seen as central to children's learning and this belief is reflected in the EYFS play-based curriculum. Therefore, Chinese children may not play in ways that we would expect in a western context. Chan emphasised the importance of educators having an awareness of theories of how children develop and '*the need to be aware of the assumptions we are making about children's development when we implement them. Moreover, we need to understand the connection between culture and development, as theories are influenced by the cultural values and beliefs system of their time*' (p 157).

- Children who have a *chronic or complex medical need* may need to take responsibility for managing their health needs at an early age. This may mean that such children show signs of greater maturity than children of similar ages. They may also develop greater levels of resilience as a consequence of the adverse effects their health condition may have upon them.

- *A minor illness*, such as the common cold, can cause a child to regress in their development as well as negatively impact on their ability to learn.

- *Special educational needs* can affect children's learning and development in countless ways. It is important that such effects are not viewed negatively and that there is a focus on what children can do, rather than on what they cannot do.

This short summary highlights just some of the factors that mean that the expectations we have of children's learning and development can and should vary. Such factors can be a positive or a negative influence so it is vital that as a practitioner you have an in-depth understanding and knowledge of the children you look after and develop your own theories of how best to promote learning and development.

Critical questions

» *Thinking of children you have worked with, are there any examples where theories are helpful to understand children's development?*

» *How can your reflections help you to develop as a theorist?*

» *Consider how you can apply the work of modern theorists to your evaluation of observations of children in your setting.*

» *How can such knowledge help you to develop your own theories about the children you care for and educate?*

The influence of theory on policy and practice

A policy is a principle or a set of rules and guidelines formulated or adopted by an organisation. Policies are also created by government and Chapter 5 gives an overview of some of the key documents and reports that you will become familiar with in your professional practice. An important example of government policy is the Early Years Foundation Stage (DfE, 2014), which is the current curriculum framework policy that is required to be followed by practitioners in settings responsible for ECEC in England. The EYFS is statutory, which means that it is a legal requirement for settings to implement the aims and principles of the framework.

Government policies, such as the EYFS, need to be adapted by practitioners to meet the individual needs of children and families in their settings. However, government policy documents do not include a rationale for the reasons for policy decisions. Therefore, it is important that practitioners have an understanding of the theories and research that have informed the policies that must be implemented. Understanding the theory can mean there is an intelligent implementation of policy and, in turn, this can mean that children have a better experience in ECEC settings. Therefore, it is important that you keep abreast of current affairs relevant to ECEC in a relevant publication for practitioners, such as *Nursery World* (see further reading).

How attachment theory has influenced current policy and practice

This section gives a detailed explanation of how attachment theory has influenced current policy and practice. The reason for focusing on attachment theory is because positive social and emotional development is critical for children in order to enable them to reach their full potential, not just in childhood, but across the age span (see Chapter 12 for more about relationships with children). John Bowlby (1969) was the first theorist to publish his beliefs about children's responses to attachment and loss. As a consequence of his work other theorists have built on Bowlby's ideas. Figure 7.3 shows a timeline of some of the theorists who have researched relationships between children and adults.

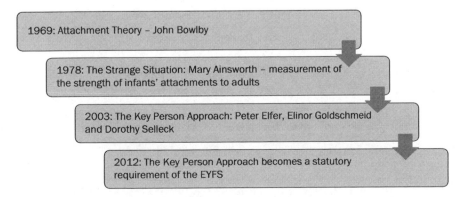

1969: Attachment Theory – John Bowlby

1978: The Strange Situation: Mary Ainsworth – measurement of the strength of infants' attachments to adults

2003: The Key Person Approach: Peter Elfer, Elinor Goldschmeid and Dorothy Selleck

2012: The Key Person Approach becomes a statutory requirement of the EYFS

Figure 7.3 *A timeline of theorists who have influenced the Key Person Approach*

The importance of their work has influenced our understanding of the need for children to have secure attachments with adults. For children in day care settings, who are separated from their parents, the role of the key person is essential for children to be able to identify an adult who they know can meet their needs and be available to them. The role of the key person is therefore vital for children's social and emotional well-being while they are apart from their parents or main carers. However, the role is especially important for vulnerable children who may have experienced poor social and emotional development because of disadvantages afforded to them by their family circumstances (see Chapter 11 for more about working with parents). Such is the importance of the key person role, the Wave Trust (2013) recommended that practitioners understand the theory behind attachment in order to be able to work effectively with young children. Knowledge of theory that is essential to achieve this aim includes that relating to:

- social and emotional development;

- age-appropriate expectations;

- findings from neuro-scientific research about early brain development.

Implications for children if practitioners do not understand theory behind policy

If you do not have a good understanding of the theory behind policy, there is a danger that the importance of such policies may be overlooked and that they are implemented in a mechanistic way. In the example given here about the theory behind the key person role, if practitioners are unaware of the need to build a positive relationship with their key children in order to help promote positive social and emotional development, there may be negative consequences for children that could continue into adulthood.

STUDENT VOICE

To illustrate how Charlotte has learned to link theories to her practice, read this letter that she wrote near the end of the second year of her degree.

Dear Student

When linking theory to practice it is of utmost importance to know that theory does not just mean people like Vygotsky, Piaget or Bruner who have developed their own concepts of how children develop, learn and play; a theory is anyone's understanding about something. Therefore, when linking theory to practice you are linking an understanding to the action; for example, a child may line up all the trains which could be described as a schema, which will then allow you as a developing professional to use this knowledge to implement activities that will enable the child to develop the schema further.

Through theory I gained an understanding of what activities will be beneficial for children's development and progression when displaying certain actions. Also, understanding theory helps you justify why you implemented certain activities; such as to test a current theory. Theory is going to become a big part of your university work so to help yourself understand the different concepts already suggested, try making flash cards with different theorists and theories on to help you during your assignment and while on placement when implementing your own activities.

Good luck with your studies.

Charlotte Forrester

Chapter reflections

This chapter has aimed to give you greater understanding of the place of theory in your practice. You are encouraged to apply criticality to how you use theories to inform your practice because it is important to bear in mind that each child is unique and there is not one theory that fits all children and families. This is why you are urged to develop your own theoretical framework in order to meet the individual needs of the children whom you care for and educate.

Further reading

Nursery World – a fortnightly publication that includes useful news reports of events, policy and research relevant to ECEC.

References

Athey, C (2007) *Extending Thought in Young Children* (2nd edition). London: Sage.

Bowlby, J (1969) *Attachment and Loss. Vol 1: Attachment*. London: Penguin.

Bruce, T (2001) *Learning Through Play: Babies, toddlers and the foundation years*. London: Hodder and Stoughton.

Chan, E Y M (2004) Narratives of Experience: How culture matters to children's development. *Contemporary Issues in Early Childhood*, 5(2): 145–59.

David, T, Goouch, K, Powell, S and Abbott, L (2003) *Birth to Three Matters: A review of the literature*. [online] Available at: webarchive.nationalarchives.gov.uk/20130401151715/https://www.education.gov.uk/publications/eOrderingDownload/RR444.pdf (accessed 1 December 2014).

Department for Education (2014) *Statutory Framework for the Early Years Foundation Stage*. London: Crown Copyright. [online] Available at: https://www.gov.uk/government/uploads/system/uploads/attachment_data/file/335504/EYFS_framework_from_1_September_2014__with_clarification_note.pdf (accessed 1 December 2014).

Elfer, P, Goldschmeid, E and Selleck, D (2003) *Key Persons in Nurseries: Building relationships for quality provision*. Abingdon: David Fulton Publishers.

Nutbrown, C (2012) *Threads of Thinking* (2nd edition). London: Sage.

Nutbrown, C, Clough, P and Selbie, P (2008) *Early Childhood Education: History, philosophy and experience*. London: Sage.

Pound, L (2005) *How Children Learn*. London: Step Forward Publishing.

Vygotsky, L (1978) *Mind in Society*. Cambridge, MA: Harvard University Press.

Wave Trust *Tackling the Roots of Disadvantage* – in collaboration with the Department for Education (2013) *Conception to Age 2 – the age of opportunity. Addendum to the Government's vision for the Foundation Years: 'Supporting Families in the Foundation Years'*. [online] Available at: www.wavetrust.org/sites/default/files/reports/conception-to-age-2-full-report_0.pdf (accessed 1 December 2014).

8 Observation, assessment and planning

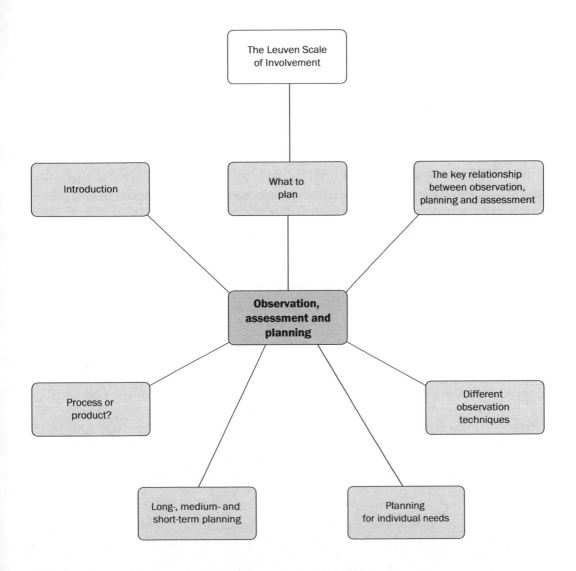

The Leuven Scale of Involvement

Introduction

What to plan

The key relationship between observation, planning and assessment

Observation, assessment and planning

Process or product?

Different observation techniques

Long-, medium- and short-term planning

Planning for individual needs

Teachers' Standards (Early Years)

The content of this chapter links to the following Early Years Teacher Award indicators:

1.1, 1.2, 1.3, 2.1, 2.2, 2.4, 2.5, 2.6, 2.7, 3.1, 3.2, 4.1, 4.2, 4.3, 4.4, 4.5, 5.1, 5.2, 5.3, 6.1, 6.2, 6.3, 8.4 and 8.6.

Introduction

You will hear the words 'Observation, planning and assessment' frequently while on placement and you may be unclear about what is expected. This chapter explains each of these terms and challenges you to question the *why* as well as the *what*. It explains the significance of involvement, using different observation techniques and sustained shared thinking, and asks you to consider whether process or product should be valued when making plans and assessing children's progress.

As a student on placement you may not be officially expected to plan for individual children's needs in the same way that an employed member of staff will be. However, it is likely that at some point in your course you will be expected to observe children and assess for learning in a hypothetical way. Wherever possible you should take the opportunity to do observations, as they become easier with practice.

The key relationship between observation, planning and assessment

When the authors began their careers, planning generally started from one of two positions:

1. what we (the teachers) were interested in; or

2. how we could contrive a topic from the national curriculum aims.

There was little observation beforehand of children's interests and it was very adult focused. The evidence from the Effective Provision of Pre-School Education (Sylva et al, 2004) shows that children learn best when there is a balance between child- and adult-led activities and an understanding of the relationship between observation, planning and assessment.

The EYFS Guidance Document, *Development Matters* (DfE, 2012) draws on this, stating that practitioners must '*understand and observe each child's development and learning, assess progress, plan for next steps*' (p 2). Much of the theory that we draw upon in practice comes from observations. For example, Jean Piaget spent a considerable time observing his own children before constructing his developmental theories. Susan Isaacs observed children in schools before proposing that children learn through play (Pound, 2005). See Chapter 7 for more about theory into practice.

Observing children is more than just watching them. We *watch* children to ensure that they are safe and not doing anything inappropriate. However, *observation* is different. Young children and babies cannot do written tests or verbalise their thoughts, so a key way of understanding them is to observe and interpret their behaviour, deciding what they need to do next in order to make good progress. In doing this we are making a judgement, or a formative assessment, of the child's progress. This informs the planning process – we need to decide whether to present more opportunities for the child to practice the task, or introduce a more challenging one, while building on their interests.

This observation, planning and assessment cycle is summarised in the EYFS as a continuous process, as shown in *Development Matters* (DfE, 2012, p 3):

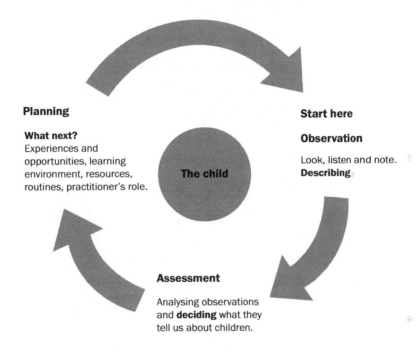

Planning

What next?
Experiences and opportunities, learning environment, resources, routines, practitioner's role.

The child

Start here

Observation

Look, listen and note.
Describing

Assessment

Analysing observations and **deciding** what they tell us about children.

Figure 8.1 *The observation, assessment and planning cycle*

Ideally, observations should be shared with parents so that a child's next steps can be followed up at home as well as in the setting (see Chapter 11 for more on working with parents).

What to plan

We plan for learning to ensure that children receive a broad and balanced curriculum; what we plan impacts on what children learn. However, excessive planning is counterproductive because for meaningful, deep learning to occur, children (and adults) need to be able to enter into a state that Mihaly Csikszentmihalyi referred to as *'flow'* (2002, cited in Fawcett, 2009, p 94).

Flow involves giving children time to become engrossed in an activity. They need to *'feel at ease, self-confident and able to act spontaneously'*, according to Ferre Laevers (1994, 2004, cited in Fawcett, 2009, p 94). The predominant characteristic of flow is concentration, with a tendency to persist. The motivation for continuing the activity is entirely intrinsic; there is a sense of time distortion (time will pass rapidly) and they feel profound satisfaction. When children are allowed to follow their own interests they often reach this state of flow, where deep and meaningful learning is developing.

Laevers was critical of over-structured approaches and developed the Leuven Scale, named after the university where he worked, to measure young children's well-being and involvement; this may be useful to you on placement in assessing how effective your planned activities are. The following is adapted from the involvement scale.

The Leuven Scale of Involvement

LEVEL 1 – NO ENGAGEMENT

Child is passive and is not focused on the activity other than possibly going through mechanical actions. They are mentally absent.

LEVEL 2 – FREQUENTLY INTERRUPTED ACTIVITY

Child engages in an indifferent manner but for half the time is not engaged in any activity, looking around at what others are doing or staring into space.

LEVEL 3 – GENERALLY CONTINUOUS ACTIVITY

Child appears to be busy but on a mundane level and does not show excitement. Easily distracted.

LEVEL 4 – CONTINUOUS ACTIVITY WITH INTENSE MOMENTS

Child is involved in activity which has real meaning for them and they are not easily distracted.

LEVEL 5 – SUSTAINED INTENSE ACTIVITY

Child is engrossed in an activity that is personally meaningful, demonstrating signs of concentration, persistence and creativity. This is where 'flow', referred to earlier, occurs.

(Fawcett, 2009)

Using the scale

Consider the following activities for children and what number on the scale of involvement they might score:

* Gather together as many items as you can find with lids, eg bottles, saucepans, small plastic storage bottles. Try to find different sizes and shapes. Separate all the tops from the bottoms and muddle them up on the floor. Ask the child to match the pieces that go together.

* Find a selection of brushes of different thicknesses (including rollers and other decorating items). Let the children paint with them, making a giant mural on the back of a roll of wallpaper. Use vocabulary such as *thick, thin, wide and narrow.*

In response to this exercise students invariably reply, 'It depends on the children', which is totally correct and reinforces the need to start planning by observing the children's interests, rather than from predetermined outcomes. It is rare to be able to devise an adult-led activity where children achieve level 5 on the involvement scale.

Critical questions

» *If children are to reach a state of flow by pursuing their own agenda what should be key components of the environment to enable them to extend their learning and not merely repeat previous experiences?*

» *To what extent should children be expected to carry out tasks that are prescribed by adults? Imagine you enjoy watching a particular soap opera – how would you feel if you were only allowed to watch the news? How does this apply to children?*

» *Which do you think is more important: that children should be able to concentrate and persevere by the time they start school, or that they can write their name and count to ten? What reasons can you give?*

Different observation techniques

When first attending placement, many students notice that practitioners often record snapshots of children's learning on sticky notes to be included in children's learning journeys. While these can provide a useful piece of the puzzle for the key person compiling the child's learning journey, they are only the tip of the iceberg in terms of informing the planning process.

Observation is the basis for planning and assessment and there are several methods of conducting observations – each one is suitable in different situations. Before undertaking your observations you should ensure that you have permission from the setting manager or head teacher and that you do not disclose any information that might make the child or the setting identifiable. You may also need to obtain permission from the child's parents. Find out the setting's policy on this before beginning.

Once you have obtained permission there is essential information that you will need to record – see below.

Name of child:	Time commenced:
Age:	Context:
Staff:	Number of children in attendance:
Description of child's play/interactions:	
Links to the EYFS:	
Characteristics of effective learning: (see pp 4–7 of *Development Matters* (DfE, 2012)).	
Next steps:	

Figure 8.2 *A sample observation record*

Below is a brief description of observational strategies that are commonly used in settings to inform planning.

- *Narrative observation*: everything that the child says and does is written down including timings. This is often compared to a 'storytelling' style, and is written in the present tense. You could add a focus – for example, if you are collecting data to inform how language develops – or proceed unfocused if you just want to get an all-round picture of a child.

- *Time sampling*: you decide an amount of time and check what the child is doing at predetermined moments; for example, you may note what a child is doing every 5 minutes for half an hour, or every 15 minutes for 2 hours. A tick list should be compiled beforehand with the categories of activity you are looking for, for example, whether the child is involved in social/parallel or solitary play, or what level of involvement they are demonstrating in their activity. This may be for several children at once, or focused on one particular child.

- *Event sampling*: this concentrates on a particular event rather than a precise period of time, for example, washing hands for snack time, or inappropriate interruptions during story time. This approach is useful if you want to investigate how to manage children's behaviour or understand why something is happening. To prepare, you should decide what material you are looking for and compile a proforma with the usual contextual details at the top, and then record the time followed by the number of events, with space for a short narrative description.

- *Checklist method*: this is more of a summative assessment than an observation and involves checking what a child, or group of children, can do, for example, which colours/shapes are known.

- *Rating scale*: this is another checklist recording what children can/cannot do, but each statement is given a rating, usually between 1 and 5, with 1 being always and 5 being never, for example, *'leaves carer without difficulty'*.

- *Tracking*: this is similar to time sampling in that it tells you which activities a child does and for how long, but instead of recording this in a narrative it is drawn on a plan of the area/room. Not only does this show what the child is interested in, but also what they avoid.

Planning for individual needs

CASE STUDY

Jakub

Jakub is three years and two months. His family has recently arrived from Poland. Jakub speaks Polish at home, but is very quiet in the setting and seems inhibited in his use of English. His key person, Stacey, undertakes a narrative observation to try to understand him better and discover a way to make him more confident at speaking English.

While observing Jakub in the book corner Stacey notices how he seeks the book *The Three Little Pigs*. She hears him say 'świnia', the Polish for pig, and then '*huff and I'll puff*'. She wonders whether Jakob is motivated to speak in English by an interest in pigs, or by the story. The next time Jakub attends she ensures that the farm set is in the continuous provision planning and the story of *The Three Little Pigs* is planned for story time.

Stacey then decides to do a time sampling observation, checking off what Jakub is doing every 5 minutes and the amount of involvement shown. She analyses the observation and finds that Jakub has not been drawn to the farm set, but has spent over 20 minutes looking at the books, where he shows an involvement score of 4. Stacey also finds that Jakub has spent 15 minutes experimenting with the musical instruments, something she had not previously noticed.

She then observes Jakub at story time as *The Three Little Pigs* is read and notices that he joins in with the repeated refrain '*I'll huff and I'll puff*' with all the other children.

Stacey realised that Jakub was not interested in pigs but enjoyed the rhythm of the repeated refrain. This was confirmed by his engagement with the musical instruments. She borrowed some dual language Polish/English story books with key repeated refrains. Jakub showed great interest in these stories and was able to teach some Polish vocabulary to Stacey. After enlisting the help of Jakub's mother, Stacey and Jakub both learned the phrases 'run, run, as fast as you can' in the others' home language. She also used the musical instruments along with her voice to teach some key routine nursery phrases, such as '*coats on*'.

Stacey talked to the other staff members about her observations and it was decided to postpone the planned topic of '*the seaside*' and plan for '*nursery rhymes*' instead. A CD was purchased of popular nursery rhymes from around the world and Jakub sang along with the ones that he recognised, first in Polish and then in English. He now not only understands more English, but has also started to use some English words.

Critical questions

» *After conducting the narrative observation what next steps would you have planned for Jakub?*

» *What knowledge did Stacey draw upon to meet Jakub's needs?*

» *How did the observations allow Stacey to understand Jakub even though they did not share a language?*

» *What might have happened if Stacey had not used these methods of observation but had instead looked for examples of progress towards the EYFS goals to record on sticky notes?*

Long-, medium- and short-term planning

While planning should be based on children's interests this does not mean that there should not be any long-term planning. When there are no plans staff can feel that they are not achieving anything and become task focused. They may, for example, sort out cupboards rather than staying tuned in to the children. When this happens the result is usually an increase in children's disruptive behaviour; another reason for ensuring planning is completed (for more on behaviour management please see Chapter 12).

Long-term planning

Long-term plans are generally completed at the beginning of the year. Typically the year is divided into equal sections (eg half terms) and the focus is decided along with the intended early learning goals. These are often related to the time of year; for example, in the autumn term there is often a focus on activities related to the season, such as trees shedding their leaves, Diwali and Bonfire Night, which will cover much of the specific area '*Knowledge of the World*'. This ensures that there is a balanced and paced approach throughout the year, both in terms of intended progression and in practicalities; for example, avoid introducing a '*mini-beasts*' topic in December when insects are hibernating.

Medium-term planning

Medium-term planning is completed just before the commencement of the planned focus, outlining in more detail the activities that may be concentrated on while drawing on the long-term plans to match up the areas of the EYFS that you intend to address. These plans are a guide to how you anticipate proceeding, but should be abandoned if not compatible with children's interests.

Short-term planning

Short-term plans are made for daily sessions and are often completed a few days in advance. They include the deployment of staff, resources that might be needed for focused activities (both indoors and outdoors) and the plans for continuous provision. The aim of continuous provision is to have resources available at all times for children, but with small changes to ensure they remain interesting. You may, for example, plan to have resources available which encourage babies to crawl. One day you may tape a long section of bubble wrap to the floor; a few days later you might put different coloured paper under the bubble wrap to maintain the babies' interest.

Process or product?

When inexperienced student practitioners are asked to plan for a child's next steps they sometimes choose an activity that values product over process. Consider the following scenarios involving student practitioners Georgina and Harpreet, who have been asked to plan for a group of two year-olds, including Anya, a child with global developmental delay, a general term used for children not developing as expected but with no definitive diagnosis:

CASE STUDY 1

Georgina

In keeping with the setting's topic of 'Under the Sea', Georgina plans an art activity where the children will paint a paper plate blue to represent the sea and allow it to dry. At the next session the children colour in pre-cut fish shapes with felt tip pens before gluing them onto the plate. Anya has difficulty understanding what she is expected to do, so to help her Georgina spreads the glue on the fish shape herself and shows Anya where to stick it on the plate. Georgina writes each child's name on their plate and then attaches them to string, which she then hangs from the ceiling with some blue and green streamers to represent seaweed and water swirling in between the painted plates.

CASE STUDY 2

Harpreet

In planning for the same topic Harpreet arranges to borrow the fish tank from the local children's centre reception area. After ensuring that the lid cannot be dislodged, she places the tank on a low table at the children's eye level and sits close by to engage with the children and extend their learning. Anya is fascinated with the fish and uses her fingers to follow the movements of the fish, tracing on the outside of the tank. She opens her mouth and tries to blow bubbles like the fish. When it is time to feed the fish Harpreet helps Anya to make a pincer grip and sprinkle some fish food onto the top of the water.

To encourage Anya to work on her pronunciation of the letters 'p' and 'b', Harpreet supports Anya as she makes the movement of the fishes' mouths opening and closing. She asks whether the continuous provision planning can be altered to include the bubbles and wands outdoors, and then supports all the children, including Anya, to blow bubbles of different sizes, asking open questions such as 'I wonder whether this star-shaped wand will make a star-shaped bubble?' and modelling small and large numbers, such as 'This big wand has only made five bubbles – how many will this little one make? Oh, I think there must be about a hundred!'

Harpreet later brings in seaweed, shells, sand, fish-tank weed and grit, placing some on trays of shallow water and some on trays with no water. She encourages the children to feel and smell the resources and models new words to extend their language.

Critical questions

»   In which scenario did the children learn more?

»   Why might Georgina have taken her approach?

» *If you were the parent/carer of Anya, which of the scenarios would you prefer her to be involved in? What are the implications of this for inclusive practice?*

» *What areas of the EYFS can you link to each scenario? Which elements of the Characteristics of Effective Learning can you identify in each scenario? How involved might the children be?*

Sustained shared thinking

In scenario 2, Harpreet spoke to the children using open-ended questions, an essential element of 'sustained shared thinking', identified as a characteristic of effective settings in the Effective Provision of Pre-school Education (EPPE) project (Sylva et al, 2004) and defined as follows:

> *Sustained shared thinking occurs when two or more individuals 'work together' in an intellectual way to solve a problem, clarify a concept, evaluate an activity, extend a narrative etc. Both parties must contribute to the thinking and it must develop and extend the understanding.*

> (p 5)

There is sometimes confusion about the 'sustained' element of this way of teaching; how long should an episode be for it to be considered sustained? There is no definite answer to this because it depends on the child's age and stage of development. It may last a few minutes with babies or weeks with older children. However, it is different to working in what Vygotsky (1978) termed the zone of proximal development (where the child's thinking is extended to the next level by an adult or more capable peer) because it should entail active involvement for both the child and the adult in an activity where there is no right or wrong answer. Consider the following case studies:

CASE STUDY 3

Abbey

Abbey sits opposite 12-month baby Hari. They both have drums in front of them. Abbey waits for Hari to bang the drum and then copies the exact rhythm played by Hari, consistently looking him in the eyes and smiling. Hari repeats his rhythmic banging and again Abbey copies his movements and sounds. Hari notices what Abbey is doing and creates a new rhythm, looking to see what Abbey will do next. He smiles broadly when she copies him again. This continues for about 5 minutes, sometimes Abbey starting a '*rhythm conversation*' for Hari to copy or extend and sometimes Hari initiating the activity.

CASE STUDY 4

Atif

Atif puts some plastic mini-beasts frozen in ice into a large tray with some water, jugs and pipettes. The children are curious about how to get the mini-beasts out of the ice. They pour water onto the ice and Atif extends their learning by asking questions such as *'what is happening to the ice?'*, *'why is there more water in the tuff spot now than there was at the beginning?'* and *'What animals like to live on the ice?'*

Critical questions

» *Which elements of these scenarios involve sustained shared thinking and which are operating in children's zone of proximal development? Give reasons for your answers.*

» *What are the implications for planning in supporting sustained shared thinking?*

» *What are the roles of practitioners in enabling sustained shared thinking?*

PRACTITIONER VOICE

Dear Student

When I first worked in a setting I wanted to be the best practitioner ever and my children would be the most advanced ever! I made sure they knew colours, letters, numbers and interesting facts, like the word 'nocturnal'. I devised tick lists to assess their ability and photocopied worksheets. I took children away from play to come and do 'work'. I thought that if they started formal learning early they would have a head start when they started school.

Some children loved these activities but others I had to bribe to come and take part. Some children failed to achieve my targets, unable to count spots on ladybirds or colour all the triangles. I realised that I was in danger of creating conditions where children felt like failures before they had even started school.

I started observing the children in their play, joining in when invited. Once I brought in an old rug and pretended it was a magic carpet. We had a brilliant time pretending to fly to the land of bouncy castles and there were more opportunities for problem solving and thinking than there ever were with worksheets.

I hope that my children will be ready for school because I have helped them love to learn; so they will still be the most advanced they can be.

My advice to you would be to ask what the children are learning from your planning. How will they be able to write a story if they have the mechanics of writing, but have nothing to write about?

Yours sincerely

Ellie

Critical questions

» *What are the advantages and disadvantages of introducing formal work in the early years?*

» *While on placement what types of activities seem to be valued? Give examples.*

» *How comfortable do you feel about engaging in children's play with no pre-set agenda? Why do you think this?*

Chapter reflections

This chapter has discussed the key points for consideration when you go into placement and begin the process of observing, planning and assessing for learning. Observations are worth taking time to master. Once you have done so you will find that they are very enlightening and ultimately very rewarding. In this chapter we have considered assessment as part of a formative process to inform planning. The next chapter considers summative assessment as part of statutory assessment.

Further reading

Palaiologou, I (2012) *Child Observation for the Early Years* (2nd edition). London: Learning Matters.

References

Department for Education (2012) *Development Matters*. [online] Available at: webarchive.nationalarchives.gov.uk/20130401151715/https://www.education.gov.uk/publications/standard/publicationDetail/Page1/DEVELOPMENT-MATTERS (accessed 1 December 2014).

Fawcett, M (2009) *Learning through Child Observation* (2nd edition). London: Jessica Kingsley Publishers.

Pound, L (2005) *How Children Learn*. London: Step Forward Publishing.

Sylva, K, Melhuish, E, Sammons, P, Siraj-Blatchford, I and Taggart, B (2004) *The Effective Provision of Pre-School Education (EPPE) Project: Findings from Pre-School to end of Key Stage 1*. [online] Available at: www.ioe.ac.uk/RB_Final_Report_3-7.pdf (accessed 1 December 2014).

Vygotsky, L (1978) *Mind in Society*. Cambridge, MA: Harvard University Press.

9 Statutory assessment

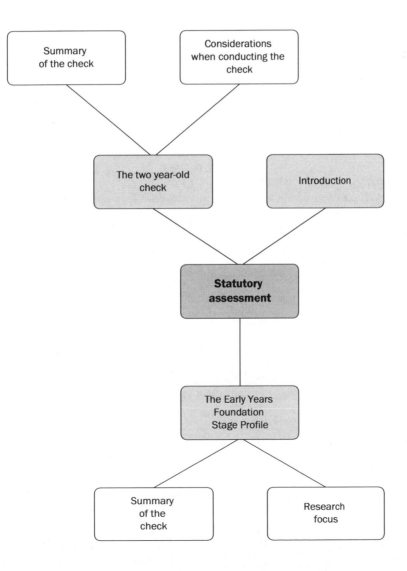

Teachers' Standards (Early Years)

The content of this chapter links to the following Early Years Teacher Award indicators:

1.2, 2.1, 2.7, 3.1, 3.3, 4.1, 4.2, 5.1, 5.2, 5.3, 5.4, 5.5, 6.1, 6.2, 6.3, 8.3 and 8.7.

Also see the Annex to the standards relating specifically to Standard 6.

Introduction

This chapter follows on from the previous chapter but focuses specifically on the two summative assessments in the EYFS:

- the two year-old check; and
- the Early Years Foundation Stage Profile (EYFSP).

Although it is unlikely that you will be expected to take responsibility for these assessments while on placement, if you are given the opportunity to contribute it would be advisable to take it because it will prepare you for when you are a professional practitioner.

The two year-old check

RESEARCH FOCUS

The two year-old check has its origins in three key documents (explored in Chapter 5):

1. *The Foundation Years: Preventing Poor Children Becoming Poor Adults* – The Field Report (Field, 2010);

2. *Early Intervention: The next steps* – The Allen Report (Allen, 2011);

3. The Tickell Review (Tickell, 2011).

The Field and Allen reports both identified that where a child was deemed to be '*at risk of failure*', intervention would be most effective if begun between the ages of two and three years old. The Tickell Review proposed that parents be given a summary of their child's progress in line with the EYFS (DfE, 2014) prime areas.

Summary of the check

The check should be carried out in the setting by someone who knows the child well, such as their key person. An aim is to identify the child's strengths as well as any potentially concerning delays in development. If these are significant, possibly indicating an underlying special educational need, then the practitioner must create a '*targeted plan*' (NCB, 2012, p 13) outlining the strategies to be employed to support the child's development, collaborating with parents and, where necessary, other professionals. Practitioners are obliged to assess children in the three Prime Areas of Learning. These are:

1. Communication and language;

2. Physical development;

3. Personal, social and emotional development.

Further information about the prime areas can be found in the EYFS (DfE, 2014). The assessment of the child is then compared with the anticipated milestones for two year-olds in *Development Matters* (DfE, 2012). Any other information is left to the discretion of the setting, but may include a general comments section for practitioners and/or parents as well as agreed next steps to support development. The timing of the check is flexible but should be completed when the child is between 24 and 36 months, ideally dovetailing with the developmental check carried out by health visitors.

Critical questions

Consider the two year-old check from various perspectives.

» *What might be the advantages and disadvantages of the two year-old check for children and families?*

» *What about for practitioners?*

» *What pros and cons might there be from a health visitor perspective?*

Considerations when conducting the check

CASE STUDY

Emma

Emma is a two and a half year-old looked-after child who has been attending nursery five mornings per week for six months. Her key person, Frazer, has been gathering evidence for Emma's two year-old check. Frazer has a good relationship with Emma and her foster carer Helen, and knows that Emma's home life is stable. Frazer has discussed the timing of the check with Helen, and agreed that now would be suitable as Emma has her health visitor check approaching.

Frazer reviews the observations conducted during the previous six months and notes how Emma moves instinctively to music. However, Emma is less confident when walking on uneven ground. Helen suggests this may be because when Emma lived with her birth mother she was often in a pushchair. Helen agrees to take Emma to places with new surfaces to negotiate and Frazer promises to ensure that Emma is encouraged to join in with daily balance activities. A meeting to review Emma's progress is set up for three months' time to decide whether to involve the Special Educational Needs Co-ordinator (SENCO). Frazer records the outcomes on the Local Authority Two Year Old Progress Check pro forma which both he and Helen sign to show their agreement (see the guidance from the National Children's Bureau about how to carry out a two year-old check in the further reading section of this chapter. The guidance includes examples of proformas that can be adapted for use in your setting.

Critical questions

» What did Frazer consider before undertaking the check?

» What is the relationship between formative and summative assessment?

» What do you consider the best way to assess a child's learning?

The Early Years Foundation Stage Profile

RESEARCH FOCUS

Research conducted into the Early Years Foundation Stage Profile (EYFSP) as part of the review of the 2008 EYFS, *The Early Years: Foundations for life, health and learning* by Dame Tickell in 2012 found that the paperwork was onerous. As a result, the government attempted to reduce the profile to make it more manageable by cutting the number of early learning goals that children needed to be assessed against to 17. However, although technically fewer, the content of the early learning goals was actually just as dense as the revised EYFS it replaced.

Summary of the check

Practitioners should draw upon formative assessments, consult parents, children and other adults involved in the child's learning to decide whether a child is meeting, exceeding or not yet meeting (emerging) the expected levels of development as outlined in *Development Matters* (DfE, 2012). The results are reported to the local authority which forwards the information to the government. It is then used to inform intervention, such as supporting summer-born children, who on average achieve lower scores in the profile than their older classmates (DfE, 2010), by, for example, suggesting part-time attendance during the first half of school's autumn term.

PRACTITIONER VOICE

Harjinder's view

Read the views of Harjinder, a Reception teacher who frequently welcomes students into her classroom.

When students are considering a research project I encourage them to discuss it with me first because it invariably involves observations of children. These are useful evidence for the EYFSP. Occasionally students focus on a subject that directly relates to the results, such as boys' writing. However, even if their research is not directly related to the profile, their observations provide worthwhile perspectives.

Critical questions

» *What other areas of student research might be relatable to the EYFSP?*

» *What role might students' observations play in maintaining a child-centred pedagogical approach?*

Chapter reflections

This chapter has given a brief insight into the summative assessment requirements of the EYFS (DfE, 2014) and their relevance for placement. Although you will probably not be responsible for conducting these checks you should be aware of what they entail. By building positive relationships with practitioners your observations can supplement others' perspectives on a child's learning.

Further reading

Dubiel, J (2014) *Effective Assessment in the Early Years Foundation Stage*. London: Sage.

References

Allen, G (2011) *Early Intervention: The next steps*. London: Crown Copyright. [online] Available at: https://www.gov.uk/government/uploads/system/uploads/attachment_data/file/284086/early-intervention-next-steps2.pdf (accessed 1 December 2014).

Department for Education (2010) *Month of Birth and Education*. Research Report DFE – RR017. [online] Available at: https://www.gov.uk/government/uploads/system/uploads/attachment_data/file/182664/DFE-RR017.pdf (accessed 1 December 2014).

Department for Education (2012) *Development Matters*. [online] Available at: webarchive.nationalarchives.gov.uk/20130401151715/https://www.education.gov.uk/publications/standard/publicationDetail/Page1/DEVELOPMENT-MATTERS (accessed 1 December 2014).

Department for Education (2014) *Statutory Framework for the Early Years Foundation Stage*. London: Crown Copyright. [online] Available at: https://www.gov.uk/government/uploads/system/uploads/attachment_data/file/335504/EYFS_framework_from_1_September_2014__with_clarification_note.pdf (accessed 1 December 2014).

Field, F (2010) *The Foundation Years: Preventing poor children becoming poor adults. The report of the Independent Review on Poverty and Life Chances*. London: Crown Copyright. [online] Available at: dera.ioe.ac.uk/14156/1/poverty-report.pdf (accessed 1 December 2014).

National Children's Bureau (NCB) (2012) *A Know How Guide: The EYFS progress check at age two.* [online] Available at: www.foundationyears.org.uk/files/2012/03/A-Know-How-Guide.pdf (accessed 1 December 2014).

Nutbrown, C (2012) *Foundations for Quality: The independent review of early education and childcare qualifications. Final Report.* Runcorn: Crown Copyright. [online] Available at: https://www.gov.uk/government/uploads/system/uploads/attachment_data/file/175463/Nutbrown-Review.pdf (accessed 1 December 2014).

Tickell, Dame C (2011) *The Early Years: Foundations for life, health and learning – an independent report on the early years foundation stage to Her Majesty's Government.* London: Crown Copyright. [online] Available at: https://www.gov.uk/government/uploads/system/uploads/attachment_data/file/180919/DFE-00177-2011.pdf (accessed 1 December 2014).

10   Working with colleagues

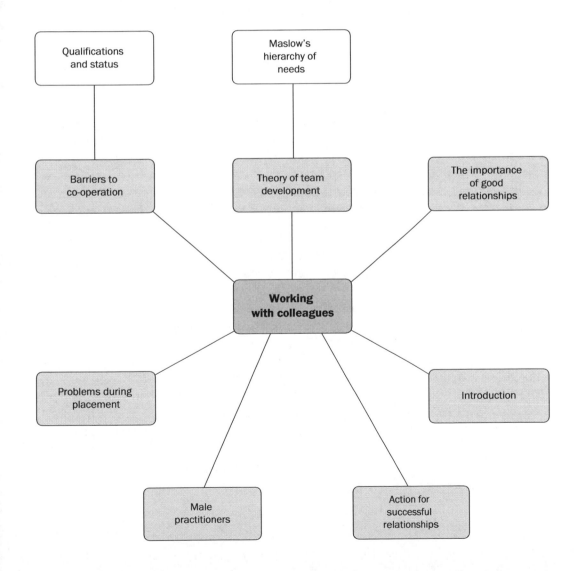

Qualifications and status

Maslow's hierarchy of needs

Barriers to co-operation

Theory of team development

The importance of good relationships

Working with colleagues

Problems during placement

Male practitioners

Action for successful relationships

Introduction

Teachers' Standards (Early Years)

The content of this chapter links to the following Early Years Teacher Award indicators:

5.5, 6.2, 8.2, 8.3, 8.4 and 8.5.

Introduction

This chapter will explain the importance of: good relationships with colleagues; the unique factors of working with other adults in early years settings; some theory on team formations; why relationships are sometimes difficult; and what you can do to make a successful contribution to team building. It will also consider the experiences men may have when integrating into predominantly female teams. It concludes with advice of what to do when placements become difficult.

The importance of good relationships

Anning and Edwards (1999), cited in Rodd (2006), recognised that working in an early years setting is as much about working with adults as it is with children when they stated, *'children's optimum development and learning are dependent on quality interpersonal relationships'* (p 68). Therefore, when you begin placement it is essential that you try to build good relationships with other practitioners, not only because it will make your placement more pleasant, but also because it will impact on the children, particularly those who have experienced insecure attachments. Adults who communicate positively with one another are good role models for these vulnerable children, supporting them in building the resilience to cope with adverse life events.

Unfortunately there will probably be some placements where you sense tension between practitioners. This can shake your confidence as you will be unaware of the cause of the tension and may assume the blame lies with you. This is unlikely to be the case; early years settings have great potential for discord as Bloom (2000, cited in Aubrey, 2007) found when interviewing early years leaders to identify the easiest and most problematic parts of their job. Many stated that they found working with adults to be the most challenging aspect of their responsibilities – *'In Early Years settings it is not uncommon to come across hurtful gossip, unkind humour, subtle insults, "tiny lies" or omissions of truth and covert pecking orders'* (Rodd, 2006, p 73). These *'toxic transactions'*, as Steiner describes them (1999, cited in Rodd, 2006, p 73), may result in despondency. This affects the children because they will react in an emotionally destructive atmosphere by becoming destructive themselves.

Barriers to co-operation

Critical questions

» *Explain the term 'in loco parentis' in your own words.*

» *To what extent is looking after children in a setting like taking on the role of a parent? To what extent is it different?*

» *Consider your own upbringing; how might this influence the way you interact with children?*

» *How might staff's experience of parenting affect the way they:*

  » *discipline children;*

  » *respond to children's different personalities;*

  » *manage the need for flexible routines;*

  » *deliver the curriculum?*

Qualifications and status

In addition to issues involving team dynamics, some less secure practitioners may feel threatened by the qualification you are seeking. The early years workforce has seen many changes in the past 20 years, some of which are described in Chapter 3.

Children aged four are four times as likely to be in a maintained setting (such as a school), which has a much higher percentage of graduate workers. For three year-olds the picture is the other way around: with 35 per cent more attending private, voluntary or independent settings (DCSF, 2008b), where the number of graduates is only 4 per cent (DCSF, 2008a). This suggests that you may encounter a different attitude towards the qualifications you aspire to, depending on the type of placement you attend.

Staff in maintained settings may be more experienced in supporting undergraduates. However, in the voluntary sector, where you are likely to be working with children aged three and under, there may be worry about the future. In 2004 the government's ten-year strategy stated that a graduate should be in every setting by 2015 (DfES, 2004). Although this was not endorsed by the Coalition Government, there may still be anxiety caused by uncertainty among staff that have worked in early years for many years but do not have the inclination or capacity to undertake additional formal qualifications.

It may be that it is what you represent, as a future graduate practitioner, rather than who you are, which causes an instinctive emotional response in some practitioners.

Critical questions

» *Consider the impact of a graduate-led profession from the perspective of:*

  1. *a level 2 practitioner with 15 years' experience;*

  2. *an apprentice;*

  3. *a level 3 room leader;*

  4. *the setting manager.*

» *How supportive might they be towards you?*

» *What could you do to win them over?*

Theory of team development

When considering the characteristics of the practitioner teams that you will encounter on placement, an understanding of the stages of team development can be helpful. At different stages of development, a team can be considered as:

* '*Forming*': the team is new, full of positive expectations. While behaviour is polite, little is actually achieved.

* '*Storming*': the novelty has worn off and there may be power struggles as the team re-negotiates goals. Little of significance is achieved.

* '*Norming*': the team know one another and are supportive. There are tacit rules and performance improves. The use of 'we' rather than 'I' Indicates that the team has reached this stage.

* '*Performing*': the team has co-ordinated working harmoniously together to achieve real results.

(Tuckman, 1965, pp 384–99)

Rodd (2006) refers to the lesser used fifth stage of '*adjourning*' or closure (p 157), which she suggests is not recognised by many leaders of settings in their anxiety to move forward and create a new team. If staff have not had the opportunity to go through the closure stage it is possible that they will be unmotivated to summon the emotional energy necessary to build new relationships.

High staff turnover could mean that the team you join when on placement has not progressed beyond the storming phase. As a new, albeit temporary member of the team, you may unwittingly unbalance precarious team dynamics. Although your potentially destabilising impact in the setting is not your fault, it is important to be self-aware and accept that you are not a passive observer of practice, even if this is what you would prefer to be.

Maslow's hierarchy of needs

When trying to establish good relationships on placement it might be helpful to consider practitioners' motivations for working. Maslow's hierarchy of needs (1970, cited in Rodd, 2006, p 87) suggests that at a basic level people have physiological needs, such as food and water. This is represented by the wages paid to practitioners. Once these needs have been met the next level, security needs, are pursued. Those on temporary contracts are not likely to have progressed beyond this. When staff have reached the third level, belonging, there is more likely to be a harmonious atmosphere, for example, staff remember each other's birthdays. In the next two levels, esteem and self-actualisation, staff seek responsibility and new knowledge.

Critical questions

»   *When staff teams are at the forming stage what level of need are they likely to be at?*

»   *How might high staff turnover affect the needs of the rest of the team?*

»   *What could you do to promote harmony?*

CASE STUDY

Beth

While on placement I was in the kitchen when a new practitioner, Becky, made herself a cup of tea. She took the teabag from the cup, walked across the floor and placed it in the bin. Another practitioner, Rosie, said, 'we don't make tea like that here; we put the tea bags into this dish to stop them dripping on the floor, then throw them away at the end of the day'. Becky didn't reply, but rolled her eyes at me behind Rosie's back.

Later, when Rosie was involved in circle time, one of the children was misbehaving. However, Becky carried on washing the paint pots even though Rosie obviously needed support.

Critical questions

»   *If you were in Beth's position what would you do while in the kitchen? During circle time?*

»   *What stage of team development might this setting be at? Why do you think this?*

Action for successful relationships

While difficult relationships can be repaired, it's always best to ensure that problems are avoided in the first place. There are some things you can do to make success more likely:

- Make sure you know the absence procedure if you must take time off. Not turning up will damage trust.

- Arrive on time and volunteer for additional tasks.

- Concentrate on the children. They are likely to create a positive focus for warring practitioners and are also the ones to lose out if relationships are not positive.

- Try to remain neutral and integrate into the routine as quickly as possible.

- Ensure that you follow the same behaviour management policy as the other staff so that they are not irritated that the children are 'wound up' by you.

- Do not slack. If the children go outside, go outside with them rather than complete paperwork indoors, whatever the weather. This will earn you respect.

PRACTITIONER VOICE

Molly

We have had a lot of students who have just stood. They can see what we're doing – for example, at lunchtime carrying the food – but they don't offer to help. They've got to throw themselves in – it's a hands-on job. If you lack confidence it's hard to put yourself out there but they've got to do it; it's amazing what can be achieved after that first step ... We do the same things day in, day out, it's so nice to have someone enthusiastic and full of fresh ideas.

Critical questions

» *Based on Molly's views of students, to what extent are they considered 'an extra pair of hands' in her setting?*

» *Make a list of specific ways you can earn practitioners' respect. How might you put these ideas into practice on your placement?*

STUDENT VOICE

Kiri

As a student I was worried it was not my place to have a sense of humour, but as I began to laugh with the other practitioners I formed relationships that supported my professional development and also enabled me to feel confident enough to offer my perspectives and ideas to the setting.

Being a student is difficult; however, getting actively involved in a setting helped me develop into the practitioner I am today.

Male practitioners

Early years practitioners are predominantly female, so if you are a male student you may feel even more self-conscious on placement. While many practitioners will welcome the new dynamic that you bring to the team, you may still face prejudice.

As a male practitioner you need to be particularly self-aware and mindful of the context into which you step. Whether you consider gender to be significant or not, *'reflective integrity'* (McDowall-Clark and Murray, 2012, p 59) will enable you to make effective connections with other practitioners in an environment where some may still view you with *'cultural unease'*, particularly if you are the first male practitioner they have encountered (Owen, 2003: Sargent, 2005, cited in McDowall-Clark and Murray, 2012, p 60), without taking any prejudices personally. Tom, in the male student practitioner's voice below, demonstrates reflective integrity by the way he has made adjustments to the language he uses to maintain positive relationships with other practitioners.

MALE PRACTITIONER VOICE

Tom

I've had to learn to speak quite differently. I've learned to use phrases such as 'It seems like ...', 'I've noticed that ...', and 'Could you maybe help me with ...?'

... I think men often use absolutes – for instance I would say, 'It is like this' – so for me it's been a matter of moving away from such a definite point of view. In female-dominated environments male language can sometimes appear aggressive, or else be misinterpreted as arrogant.

(McDowall-Clark and Murray, 2012, p 60)

Critical questions

» *How has critically reflecting changed Tom's behaviour?*

» *Do you agree that gender influences the hidden messages in our language? Why?*

» *To what extent do you think the male experience of the early years sector might be similar to a female's and how might they be different?*

Problems during placement

No placement will be perfect and all will present some challenges for you to overcome. However, remember that settings will never adapt to you, it's up to you to adapt to the setting. If you do have difficulties there are steps you can take to still get the most from your placement.

- Keep a positive frame of mind. Disarm negative people with a smile!

- Do not get drawn into cliques and power struggles; try to remain neutral.

- Make positive comments about good practice. This will reassure insecure practitioners that you are not being judgemental.

- If you have a problem with a member of staff talk to your mentor. Avoid *'telling tales'* and gossiping.

- When you speak to your mentor ensure it is at an agreed time and not when they are on a break or in the corridor.

- Be professional when discussing your difficulties. Do not accuse or belittle anyone and suggest solutions as well as asking for support.

- If the difficulty is with your placement mentor talk to your university tutors.

- It is never an option to walk out of a placement. This makes you look very unprofessional, and remember, you can learn from bad practice as well as good.

Chapter reflections

Good relationships among colleagues are important for the well-being of both staff and children but, for various reasons, they might not be established in your placement setting. Being aware of possible factors contributing to this situation will enable you to respond in a way that adds to a harmonious atmosphere, resulting in a rewarding and successful placement.

Further reading

Reed, M and Callan, S (2010) *Reflective Practice in the Early Years.* London: Sage.

References

Aubrey, C (2007) *Leading and Managing in the Early Years.* London: Sage.

Department for Children, Schools and Families (2008a) Childcare and Early Years Providers Survey 2007. [online] Available at: https://www.gov.uk/government/uploads/system/uploads/attachment_data/file/191537/DCSF-RR047.pdf (accessed 1 December 2014).

Department for Children, Schools and Families (2008b) *Provision for Children Under Five Years of Age in England.* [online] Available at: webarchive.nationalarchives.gov.uk/20130401151655/http://www.education.gov.uk/researchandstatistics/statistics/allstatistics/a00193352/provision-for-children-under-five-years-of-age-in- (accessed 1 December 2014).

Department for Education and Skills (2004) *Choice for Parents, the Best Start for Children: A ten year strategy for childcare.* [online] Available at: webarchive.nationalarchives.gov.uk/20130401151715/http://www.education.gov.uk/publications/eOrderingDownload/HMT-991151.pdf (accessed 1 December 2014).

McDowall-Clark, R and Murray, J (2012) *Reconceptualizing Leadership in the Early Years*. Maidenhead: Open University Press.

Rodd, J (2006) *Leadership in Early Childhood* (3rd edition). Maidenhead: Open University Press.

Tuckman, B W, (1965) Developmental Sequence in Small Groups. *Psychological Bulletin*, 63(6): 384–99.

11 Working with parents

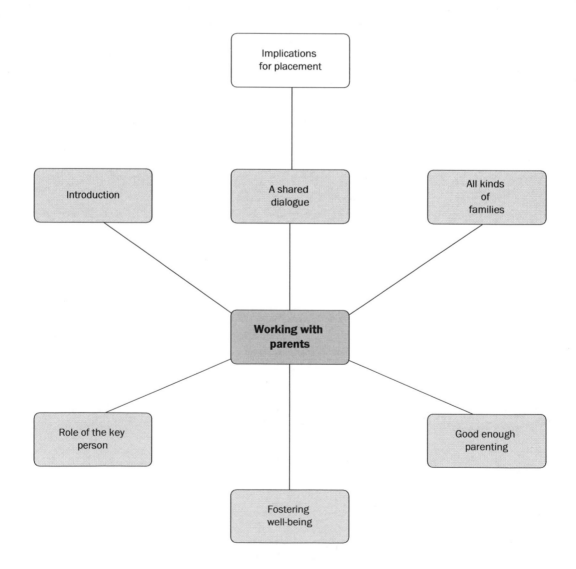

Teachers' Standards (Early Years)

The content of this chapter links to the following Early Years Teacher Award indicators:

2.3, 2.4, 2.7, 3.1, 4.3, 5.5, 6.2, 6.3, 8.1 and 8.3.

Introduction

Working with parents is consistently cited by students as an area for development at every stage of their course, and you are probably no different. This chapter outlines some tensions for practitioners working with parents in terms of power balance, the rationale for working with parents, the need to respect the diverse range of families and the role of the key person in building positive relationships and fostering well-being. The term 'parent' is used to refer to anyone who has taken on this role.

Some settings have a student/parent policy that you should refer to before interacting with parents. Reasons for this are explained later in the chapter.

Research focus

Working collaboratively with parents is an accepted requirement of early years practice (DfE, 2014). However, research by Morrow and Malin (2004) found that the rhetoric and the reality of working in partnership with parents were sometimes different. Citing Pease (2002), they note that a defining characteristic of being a professional is holding specialist knowledge, which brings inherent power. In the early years, however, if the aim is to flatten power hierarchies (McDowall-Clark and Murray, 2012), and work with parents as equals, this may bring challenges for practitioners' professional identity.

While the practitioners in Morrow and Malin's research were pleased when parents said they communicated 'on the same level' with them (p 175), one of the practitioners reflected on the personal implications of this, stating that although the relationship with parents was 'more real', for her it also brought a 'loss of status' adding '... but for me I think that's all right' (p 170).

These tensions will be felt to a greater or lesser degree by the practitioners with whom you work on placement. The extent to which they think it's 'all right' will determine whether the partnership they forge with parents is genuinely equal or tokenistic.

Critical question

» *To what extent do you agree that when practitioners empower parents to work in equal partnership there are implications for their professional status?*

All kinds of families

Article Two of the United Nations Convention on the Rights of the Child (UNCRC, 1989) states that children have the right not to be discriminated against. This includes implicit discrimination associated with less conventional families, such as same-sex parents, teenage parents, traveller parents, drug-dependent parents or parents of large families.

The EYFS (DfE, 2014) was specifically designed to provide partnership working with parents and equality of opportunity (p 5). One of the overarching principles relates to the relationship between children, parents and practitioners:

> children learn and develop well in **enabling environments,** in which their experiences respond to their individual needs and there is a strong partnership between practitioners and parents and/or carers.

(p 6)

While most people in principle believe that families from all sections of society should not be discriminated against, when faced with new situations it can be difficult to remain neutral. Consider the following case study.

CASE STUDY

Anita

Anita has undertaken a placement at a children's centre. A young single mother, Holly, and her four year-old son, Sam, have been referred to the children's centre by their social worker. Holly's attendance is sporadic and Sam often arrives looking grubby and hungry. Sam is very small for his age and wears clothes that are unsuitable for the season. Anita, however, notices that Holly has the latest mobile phone and designer trainers.

One day Sam arrives with his arm in a sling and a gash on his head. While playing in the street unsupervised he fell from a tree, fractured his wrist and suffered concussion. Holly had been drinking so was unable to take him to casualty, but phoned her mother, who drove them.

Anita is shocked that Holly is allowed to continue to care for Sam. She feels that if Sam had been taken into care this could have been prevented.

Critical questions

» Consider Sam's home situation and try to identify the strengths, risks and points to check.

» What do Sam and Holly need from the children's centre?

» If you were Anita what would you do in this situation in terms of working for the best outcomes for Sam?

Good enough parenting

The concept of good enough parenting is attributed to Donald Winnicott (1964, cited in Ramaekers and Suissa, 2012). He proposed that it was unrealistic to expect parents to be perfect all the time and that the vast majority were doing their best for their children. Considering what we know from research about the importance of love on the shaping of a baby's brain (Gerhardt, 2004), it could be argued that good enough parenting is where attachment and security are consistently fostered. If these are in place then the basis for future good mental health is established (for further information on attachment theory see Chapter 7).

Sometimes parenting is not good enough; when making difficult decisions the needs of the child should be 'paramount' (Children Act, 1989).

Critical questions

» Having read the section on good enough parenting, have your views on Sam's situation altered?

» Would you consider Holly's parenting to be 'good enough'?

» At what point would you decide that parenting was not good enough? How have your values underpinned this decision?

Fostering well-being

Working with parents has been incorporated into early childhood curricula in many other countries. New Zealand's early years curriculum, Te Whariki (Ministry of Education, 1996), for example, is underpinned by aspirations for every child, one of which is to feel a sense of 'belonging'. To a child, knowing that both they and their family belong in the setting increases their well-being; essential for learning and development.

In practice this means that you should encourage learning that starts from the experiences of home life. For example, the use of a family's home language should be encouraged in the setting, extended family members' names and traditions should be remembered. When you are planning activities think about how you can link the setting to the wider world of the child through familiar people, images, objects, sounds and smells from home, before going on to introduce those that are different. Try to create opportunities for families and practitioners to share time together, for example, at a barbecue or on a trip. When families feel they belong in the setting they are more likely to share insights into their child's learning at home. If parents are earnestly listened to then practitioners can work with them to achieve the best possible outcomes for children.

Role of the key person

The Te Whariki approach is an example of partnership working between parents and practitioners at its best. This is also the aim of settings in England where there is a statutory obligation to assign each child a key person, whose role is defined in the EYFS as:

to help ensure that every child's learning and care is tailored to meet their individual needs ... to help the child become familiar with the setting. Offer a settled relationship for the child and build a relationship with the parents.

(DfE, 2014, p 21)

According to Elfer et al (2012), properly implementing the key person approach benefits all involved. For babies and young children there is someone in the setting who values them while they are away from home. Parents are likely to experience *'peace of mind'* (p 23) as they leave their child with someone who is committed to them, plus the chance to share the sometimes stressful task of raising a child. For the key person, feeling that they really matter to the family and the child also brings a great sense of well-being.

A shared dialogue

If every child's learning is to be tailored to their individual needs to enable the child to discover the world from the familiar base of home, then a shared dialogue with parents is essential.

Hedges et al (2011), citing Gonzalez (2005), described the unique experiences that children bring from home as *'funds of knowledge'* (p 186). In researching how children's interests were incorporated into the planning, the authors found that practitioners tended to assume that they knew what children were interested in, providing everyday play resources because their observations showed that the children engaged with them. One child cooked extensively at home with her mother and recreated this by engaging in sand and water play in the setting. The practitioners noted that she enjoyed the sand and water, but did not follow up further to learn about her experiences of cooking at home – the likely motivation behind her engagement with sand and water. Knowing this would potentially have added more opportunities for meaningful learning.

The authors found that children had many more 'funds of knowledge' than they were given credit for. They were, for example, aware of household routines such as cleaning and cooking, managing budgets, parental occupations, parents and grandparents' interests, talents and leisure activities. While some confident children often naturally discuss their home life, the lives of quieter or non-verbal children may be largely unknown. It is only by building informal, trusting relationships with parents over time that practitioners can learn about and then build on the 'funds of knowledge' that children have.

Critical questions

» *What do parents know about their child that practitioners do not?*

» *What do practitioners know about the child that parents do not?*

» *How far do you think children's individual interests should be catered for? Should the setting encourage 'educational' activities, or should interests in popular television shows, for example, be planned for?*

Implications for placement

PRACTITIONER VOICE

When I managed a setting I knew how difficult students found talking to parents. I encouraged them to share observations when parents came to collect their child. One student fed back to a mother, Lisa, as she collected her son Josh, 'All he's done today is walk round the edges of the room. He hasn't played with any of the toys or children. To be honest, I think he was a bit bored …'

It was at this point that I appreciated why some settings did not allow students to talk to parents. Josh's behaviour was being monitored by the setting SENCO. He was later diagnosed with Asperger's Syndrome, and building a positive relationship with Lisa was crucial in supporting her in coming to terms with Josh's condition. Sometimes honesty can be confused with unnecessary bluntness.

Critical questions

»   *If you were the student in this situation what would you have done?*

»   *What could you do while on placement to establish a mutually beneficial relationship with parents?*

»   *In this scenario the practitioners talked to parents at the end of the day about the child's experiences. What other opportunities for parents and practitioners to communicate have you witnessed?*

»   *Can you think of other ideas to share information?*

PARENT VOICE

When we leave Ella with you we need to know that you have her best interests at heart. When something new becomes important we want to know that you are interested. We want you to remember the important things that we share with you; that you are hearing AND listening.

We know that you are bound by lots of rules and red tape. We know that there is a curriculum that you have to follow and that there is lots of paperwork that you have to complete. However, when you use jargon it sometimes leaves us in a cold sweat!

We recognise that it is really important to get involved during Ella's time with you. We want to find out what she has been doing and how these opportunities fit into her learning and development. However, we also need you to recognise that we are very busy with work and with family life. Please try to give us as much notice as possible if you need us to take time off work. We don't WANT to miss sports day, the Christmas play or an opportunity to stay and play but we need you to understand that it is sometimes not possible to do everything. Please don't think any less of us for having to make difficult choices and sometimes having to say no.

Critical questions

» What is the difference between hearing and listening?

» What jargon might practitioners use? What might be the effect if practitioners use jargon when building relationships?

» How might parents be pressurised by government policy to make choices between the two competing priorities of being a working parent or being a full-time parent?

Chapter reflections

This chapter has focused on working with parents as it relates to your practice. Building positive relationships with parents enables more meaningful planning for children and when problems are presented to children in meaningful contexts, they are much more likely to accomplish their potential.

Further reading

Ward, U (2013) *Working with Parents in the Early Years* (2nd edition). London: Sage.

References

Children Act (1989) [online] Available at: www.legislation.gov.uk/ukpga/1989/41/section/1 (accessed 1 December 2014).

Department for Education (2014) *Statutory Framework for the Early Years Foundation Stage.* London: Crown Copyright. [online] Available at: https://www.gov.uk/government/uploads/system/uploads/attachment_data/file/335504/EYFS_framework_from_1_September_2014__with_clarification_note.pdf (accessed 1 December 2014).

Elfer, P, Goldschmied, E and Selleck, D Y (2012) *Key Persons in the Early Years: Building relationships for quality provision in early years settings and primary schools.* Oxon: Routledge.

Gerhardt, S (2004) *Why Love Matters: How affection shapes a baby's brain.* London: Routledge.

Hedges, H, Cullan, J and Jordan, B (2011) Funds of Knowledge as a Conceptual Framework for Children's Interests. *Journal of Curriculum Studies*, 23(2): 185–285.

McDowall-Clark, R and Murray, J (2012) *Reconceptualising Leadership in the Early Years.* Maidenhead: Open University Press.

Ministry of Education (1996) *Te Whariki Early Childhood Curriculum.* Wellington: Learning Media Ltd. [online] Available at: www.educate.ece.govt.nz/~/media/Educate/Files/Reference%20Downloads/whariki.pdf (accessed 1 December 2014).

Morrow, G and Malin, N (2004) Parents and Professionals Working Together: Turning the rhetoric into reality. *Early Years: An International Research Journal*, 24(2): 163–77.

Ramaekers, S and Suissa, J (2012) *The Claims of Parenting: Contemporary philosophies and theories in education 4.* London: Springer.

12 Relationships with children

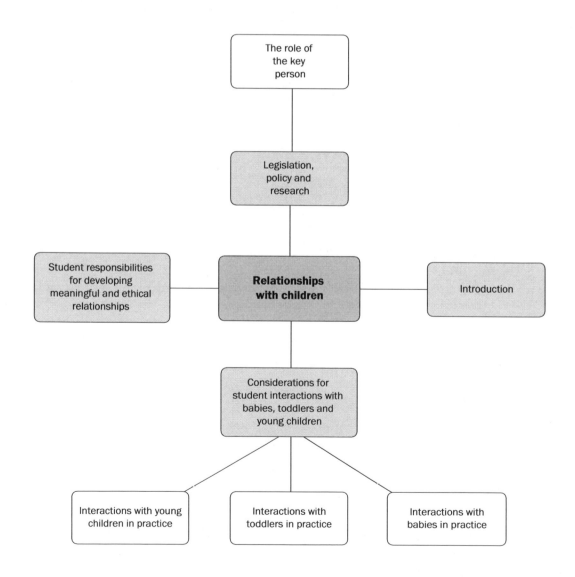

The role of
the key
person

Legislation,
policy and
research

Student responsibilities
for developing
meaningful and ethical
relationships

**Relationships
with children**

Introduction

Considerations for
student interactions with
babies, toddlers and
young children

Interactions with young
children in practice

Interactions with
toddlers in practice

Interactions with
babies in practice

Teachers' Standards (Early Years)

The content of this chapter links to the following Early Years Teacher Award indicators:

1.3, 2.2, 2.3, 2.5, 2.6, 2.7, 3.1, 5.2, 8.3, 8.4 and 8.6.

Introduction

This chapter explores relationships you will form with babies, toddlers and young children while on professional placement. Practitioners work with parents in order to develop relationships with children in early years settings and Chapter 11 addressed your role in working with parents. The approaches you develop to promote positive relationships and interactions with children will be influenced by the age and stage of development of those children. This reinforces the need for you to have in-depth knowledge of child development so that you can consider the changes in interactions that may occur as a child develops through the stages. It is also important that you are aware of legislation, policy and research about the importance of relationships with children aged 0–5 years. In this chapter you will read about Maryum and Lauren's experiences of working with children; their contributions will help you to reflect upon some of the considerations and challenges of developing appropriate relationships with children.

Legislation, policy and research

Positive relationships for babies and young children are vital for their emotional and social well-being in childhood and across the lifespan. The pioneering work of John Bowlby (see Chapter 7) resulted in what we now refer to as attachment theory, which was the starting point for research regarding early relationships. Building on Bowlby's findings neuroscientific research has also confirmed the need for babies to have warm interactions with adults. For children in early years settings who may be away from their parents or carers for long periods of time, it is important that they have an adult who knows them and can help them to feel loved and understood. This point is reflected in the Wave Trust and Department for Education (2013) report that states that:

> Practitioners should be able to build warm, responsive and sustained relationships with young children confirmed by visual, auditory and physical contact.
>
> (p 64)

Government policy recognised the significance of the research findings when the role of the key person was introduced in the EYFS (2008), which then became statutory in the 2012 revised EYFS.

The role of the key person

The EYFS has a statutory requirement that each child in day care settings is assigned a key person. The EYFS description of the role is:

to help ensure that every child's care is tailored to meet their individual needs ... to help the child become familiar with the setting, offer a settled relationship for the child and build a relationship with their parents.

(DfE, 2014, p 21)

A child's key person is designed to be the person that babies can regard as a safe harbour in a busy day care setting, a person to whom they can reach out for reassurance and affirmation. The need for children to have a safe harbour concurs with Bowlby's theory of attachment and it is vital that they have a special relationship with an adult when they are away from their home and family. However, the realities of implementing the policy can be complex. For example, a key person will have several children in their key group, therefore from a practical point of view it can be difficult to ensure that practitioners and children are always attending the setting at the same time.

For more information about the role of the key person, see Elfer et al (2011).

Critical questions

»   *How have you observed the role of the key person implemented in settings?*

»   *What are the advantages and disadvantages of the key person approach?*

Student responsibilities for developing meaningful and ethical relationships

As a student you will not be a key person for children in your setting, however, it is still part of your responsibility to develop meaningful relationships with them. To achieve this you should interact with them to develop two-way communication. However, for a student it can be challenging to understand what is an appropriate amount of interaction and there are considerations and challenges to be aware of, both from your point of view and from the child's.

As with all people, some children are easier to develop relationships with than others. However, it is ethical practice to ensure that you aim to develop a positive relationship with all children, remembering that, as Nutbrown (1996) states, all children deserve the opportunity to have good relationships in early childhood and to be treated equally by practitioners:

Not just children who are easy to work with, obliging, endearing, clean, pretty, articulate, capable, but every child – respecting them for who they are, respecting their language, their culture, their history, their family, their abilities, their needs, their name, their ways and their very essence.

(p 54)

There are many reasons why it can be easier to develop relationships with some children than others. Some of these may relate to characteristics of individual children, as implied in Nutbrown's words. It is important to recognise your own biases that may be a barrier to developing positive relationships. For example, you may not find it easy to work with babies, or you may feel self-conscious about interacting with very young children who have limited spoken language. By reflecting on your practice in relation to interacting with babies and children you should be able to identify your barriers and then work towards improving your skills.

Considerations for student interactions with babies, toddlers and young children

Interactions with babies in practice

As with every other child it is important that through observations you get to know children and learn the best ways of interacting with each child. Some of how you interact and relate with children will depend on their age and stage of development. It must be remembered that children are unique and some will require a lot of physical interaction in order to feel secure. Others may dislike physical contact, for instance children with autism may not like to be held. Babies often like to be physically held in order to feel secure and if they are not held, they may express their distress by crying. However, practices can vary in how babies are responded to. Maryum's experience in the baby room illustrates this point.

CASE STUDY

Maryum

Maryum is in the final year of her early childhood degree and is in the second week of her placement in the baby room. Two of the babies are fractious and they find it difficult to settle down. They cry inconsolably and are only soothed when picked up and held, after which they start to show interest in their surroundings and become engaged. At the start of her placement, Maryum found that by picking the babies up and engaging them with the contents of a treasure basket, not only were the babies happier, but there was also a calmer atmosphere in the baby room because everybody was less stressed. The practitioner who had been covering for the room leader was pleased with the work Maryum had done and staff commented positively on the changes in the babies' behaviour. However, when the baby room leader returned from annual leave a tension developed in the room.

The room leader believed that the babies were being 'spoilt' and should be left to cry so that they did not expect to be picked up 'all the time'. She showed her disapproval towards Maryum when she responded to the babies by tutting and glaring at Maryum when she picked the babies up. The room leader's disapproving behaviour escalated when she started to voice her belief to everybody in the room about how spoilt the babies were and how picking them up was unfair to the other babies. The situation was posing an ethical dilemma for Maryum because she knew from observing the babies that they were happier when they had physical contact to reassure them. Her knowledge of attachment theory and other research (Musgrave, 2010) confirmed that babies need a safe base from which to explore their world. In this instance, the safe base was initial physical contact and positive interaction with Maryum as well as access to interesting activities, such as the treasure basket. The other practitioners in the room were young and relatively inexperienced and were confused by the conflicting practices that Maryum and the room leader advocated. Maryum realised that the situation was untenable and needed to be addressed.

Critical questions

» Consider the possible effects or implications of the above situation from each of the following people's perspectives:

   a) the babies;

   b) the other practitioners;

   c) the room leader;

   d) Maryum.

» What are the possible solutions to addressing the practice of not picking babies up and interacting appropriately with the babies?

» How could Maryum lead on changing practice to address the approach to interactions with babies?

» Drawing on modern attachment theories and research – for example, see Page (2011) and Page et al (2013) – summarise the main points of the importance of physical and emotional interaction with babies.

Interactions with toddlers in practice

Toddlers often continue to interact in a physical way, wanting to be held and sat on your lap. However, as their language and level of independence increases, the amount of physical contact they require may decrease.

Through observation and working with children's key persons you will get to know the children in your setting and be able to judge their likes and dislikes. It is important to remember that all children are given attention of the 'right' sort (meaning attention that acknowledges their right to have their voice heard). The right sort of attention from practitioner to child helps the child to maintain their secure base so they feel emotionally capable of engaging with their learning in their setting.

You may sometimes find it difficult to gauge the right amount of attention, especially if a child is drawn to you and initiates an attachment. Conversely, sometimes, you may be drawn to a particular child and can enjoy the affection which may be manifested in hugs and cuddles. However, it is important that children do not have their engagement with activities interrupted by frequent demonstrations of affection by adults. It may also be the case that you are concerned about appearing to be giving children 'too much' attention. There are many reasons for such concerns, but students most commonly report that they are worried that a child may become overly reliant on them.

You may also be concerned about showing favouritism to a child and try to divert the attentions in order to appear to be fair. Some students, especially males, become worried about demonstrating physical contact with children because of concerns relating to safeguarding issues (see Chapter 4). Such concerns can mean that you avoid physical contact with children. Nevertheless, this is also inappropriate, especially for toddlers who may still require emotional comfort through physical contact.

The aim of students working with children for what may be a short period of time is to develop positive relationships that involve a healthy balance between physical and verbal interaction. However, it is important that your feelings are acknowledged because it is likely that you will experience a sense of loss when you leave a setting and are no longer working with children to whom you have become attached. Simon was a participant in the research for the Master's dissertation of one of the authors of this book, Jackie Musgrave, and he demonstrated his level of involvement and attachment to the child on whom he had conducted a longitudinal study. Several months after leaving the setting he said: '*I can remember everything about his routine and what he needed.*' Simon looked at the clock in the classroom, and smiling reflectively continued: '*He would be having his morning nap now. I really miss him.*' Simon's words convey a sense of sadness at the loss of his relationship with the child he got to know so well. His words also highlight a reality of life, which is that professional relationships between early years educators and children can involve strong emotions. Jools Page describes such feelings as '*professional love*' (2011, p 192) and it is important that such emotions are acknowledged, rather than suppressed, and that you are supported in your placement, and by your academic tutor, to manage your feelings.

Interactions with young children in practice

As children become older and learn language, interactions are likely to become more verbal and less physical. Lauren has written a letter which reflects her approach and experience of interaction with such children.

STUDENT VOICE

Putting it into practice

Dear Student,

As students on placement we have a unique and important position, especially with regard to interacting with young children. Often teachers and practitioners, as much as they would love to spend all day interacting with the children, have very long 'to do' lists and responsibilities that mean they can't always spend the amount of quality time with children that they would like. Although we may have specific tasks to think about and be given jobs to do, we often have the opportunity to stop, observe and listen to children and spend time with a child who might need a bit of extra support or simply a listening ear. During my placements I have had the privilege to be invited by children to play their games and listen to their stories. I would like to encourage you to take the time to interact with the children that you meet at different settings. Here are a couple of my 'top tips' – things that I have found helpful regarding interacting with young children on the placements that I had during my three years as a student.

1. Learn every child's name as soon as you can. I try to challenge myself to learn all the children's names on the first day of a new placement. I practice them while the children are sat down on the carpet during the register or from pictures on classroom walls. I might look a bit strange but I've found that, as well as impressing children ('How do you know my name?!'), it is the first step towards showing them you value them as individuals and that you want to get to know who they are.

2. Listen and observe. A big part of interaction is listening. Listening to what children want to tell you then respectfully asking questions can tell you so much about them. Learning their interests is important. It helps them to feel valued, it gives you a greater understanding of who they are, which then in turn helps you to discover how they learn. You can adapt activities based on interactions with children to suit their preferences that, in my experience, has always meant they are more motivated and enjoy what you have planned more. As 'outsiders', at least initially, we can sometimes see things that others, who are there every day, might not be able to spot. By listening to children and really observing, we might be able to come alongside an individual who needs some encouragement or we might see a way to extend their learning that has not been spotted before.

3. Don't be embarrassed. If you are fortunate enough to be invited into a child's play narrative, don't hold back! When I started my placements I think I sometimes felt a bit awkward or silly when children invited me to join their games. Now I occasionally take a step back and realise I'm wearing a cone for a 'builder's hat' and pretending to hammer a sideboard with a toy telephone – but that it doesn't matter. The children are our priority and so it doesn't matter if we look a bit strange sometimes. When it is appropriate and we are invited into play, there are so many opportunities. In these moments there are great learning opportunities for both us and them in many different areas. For example, in the case of the 'building' play narrative I mentioned previously, this might be a language learning opportunity. I might say 'I really need four bricks over here' which would then be a numeracy learning opportunity, we could then draw four bricks or write a list on a piece of paper of building materials we needed. During child-initiated play there are any number of different learning opportunities if we are brave enough to let go of our 'adult role'.

Interacting with children has taught me more about working with them than any other aspect of my degree. They are the experts on themselves and interaction is the key to learning a vast range of different things.

I wish you all the best with your future placements.

Lauren Sylvester

Critical questions

Consider the student voice feature above.

» *How does Lauren's practice reflect the Wave Trust's statement that 'practitioners should be able to build warm, responsive and sustained relationships with young children confirmed by visual, auditory and physical contact' (p 64)?*

» *How are Lauren's values and principles of ethical practice in relation to her interactions with young children conveyed in her letter?*

» *What are the theories that underpin her practice?*

» *How can Lauren's account of her practice help her to manage children's behaviour?*

Consider this chapter as a whole. Reflect on how you develop relationships with toddlers and consider how you can work with other practitioners to judge the following:

» *How much attention do you give to each child?*

» *What is the 'right' and 'wrong' amount and type of attention?*

» *What are the boundaries to interaction and your relationship with children?*

» *How are you going to manage your own feelings about relationships when it comes to leaving your placement?*

Chapter reflections

This chapter has reinforced the need for positive relationships with babies, toddlers and young children. It has also highlighted the complexities that you may need to consider when interacting with children. There are not always straightforward answers to some of the complex situations that you may encounter. However, it is important that you learn how to develop relationships that are healthy for children and for you. Chapter 13 offers you some practical suggestions of how to manage the end of your placement and the consequent ending of your relationships with children.

Further reading

Elfer, P, Goldschmied, E and Selleck, D Y (2011) *Key Persons in the Early Years: Building relationships for quality provision in early years settings and primary schools.* Oxon: David Fulton Books.

Page, J, Clare, A and Nutbrown, C (2013) *Working with Babies and Children from Birth to Three* (2nd edition). London: Sage.

References

Department for Education (2014) *Statutory Framework for the Early Years Foundation Stage.* London: Crown Copyright. [online] Available at: https://www.gov.uk/government/uploads/system/uploads/attachment_data/file/335504/EYFS_framework_from_1_September_2014__with_clarification_note.pdf (accessed 1 December 2014).

Elfer, P, Goldschmied, E and Selleck, D Y (2011) *Key Persons in the Early Years: Building relationships for quality provision in early years settings and primary schools.* Oxon: David Fulton Books.

Musgrave, J (2010) Holding the Baby. *Nursery World.* 16 September. London: Haymarket Publications.

Nutbrown, C (ed) (1996) *Respectful Educators – Capable Learners: Children's rights and early education.* London: Sage.

Page, J (2011) Do Mothers Want Professional Carers to Love Their Babies? *Journal of Early Childhood Research,* 9(3): 310–23.

Page, J, Clare, A and Nutbrown, C (2013) *Working with Babies and Children from Birth to Three* (2nd edition). London: Sage.

Wave Trust *Tackling the Roots of Disadvantage* – in collaboration with the Department for Education (2013). *Conception to Age 2: The age of opportunity. Addendum to the Government's vision for the Foundation Years: 'Supporting Families in the Foundation Years'.* [online] Available at: www.wavetrust.org/sites/default/files/reports/conception-to-age-2-full-report_0.pdf (accessed 1 December 2014).

13 Reflecting on and writing about placement

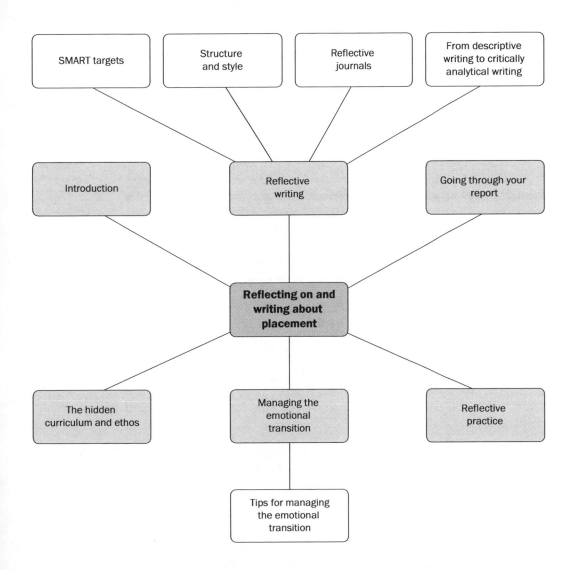

- SMART targets
- Structure and style
- Reflective journals
- From descriptive writing to critically analytical writing
- Introduction
- Reflective writing
- Going through your report
- **Reflecting on and writing about placement**
- The hidden curriculum and ethos
- Managing the emotional transition
- Reflective practice
- Tips for managing the emotional transition

Teachers' Standards (Early Years)

The content of this chapter links to the following Early Years Teacher Award indicators:

4.5 and 8.6.

Introduction

This final chapter addresses some key aspects linked to the end of placement, such as going through your report and managing your feelings, but also how to begin to reflect and critically analyse your practice in order to set targets for your continuing professional development. An important area that is often overlooked is that of the hidden curriculum and ethos. How to identify these elusive features in your specific setting is explained. Finally, advice is given about how to structure your writing and set suitable targets for an action plan.

Managing the emotional transition

You are likely to have mixed emotions when leaving placement and it is important that you carefully manage your relationships with children right from the start and are prepared for the feelings that you, the children and other staff may experience when you leave.

You may have built up a particularly strong relationship with a child on placement and this will undoubtedly boost your self-esteem. However, although you know that you will be leaving after a period of time, the child does not, and your sudden departure may cause them some trauma, particularly if they have experienced adult abandonment previously.

Tips for managing the emotional transition

- Be aware of the amount of time that you spend working one-to-one with a child, ideally sharing your attention with all the children equally.

- After interacting with babies always return them to their key person so that consistent attachment is maintained.

- When you start working with children introduce yourself and explain that you have come to play with them for a while.

- At the end of activities state that you have enjoyed playing and that you will remember the fun you had together even when you are not there and they cannot see you.

- Send the children and staff separate cards. In the staff card mention what you have learned from their practice. In the children's one mention some happy memories you shared.

Critical questions

» How might personal gratification get in the way of ethicality in terms of attachment in relationships with children?

» How might you alter your approach for different age groups?

Going through your report

Receiving your placement report can be nerve-racking but it will be more beneficial to you if you make an appointment to discuss it with your mentor. This will give them the opportunity to clarify their remarks, which is especially important if there are any negative comments. Remember, there is always something you can do to improve, and constructive feedback about areas for improvement can help you to do so.

CASE STUDY

Chris

I anticipated receiving a good report from my mentor as I felt that I had built good relationships with the children and had been friendly but not disrespectful with the staff. I had always been punctual and had volunteered to sell raffle tickets at the end of term Teddy Bears' picnic.

I was pleased with most of the report but in the 'advice for improvement' section my mentor had suggested that I should keep the setting tidier. I was disappointed, but when my mentor talked it through with me she explained that tidying up after activities that I had initiated, rather than assuming someone else would clear resources away, would endear me to the staff team in my next placement, enabling me to integrate with them more effectively.

Looking back I'm grateful to her for giving me this feedback because I did become much more aware of how I could contribute to keeping the environment organised and efficient on my subsequent placements. In fact, in my next report this was noted as a strength.

Reflective practice

As you make the transition to becoming a professional practitioner you will undoubtedly hear the term 'reflective practice'. Reflective practice is most often linked to John Dewey (1859–1952) and Donald Schön (1930–97). In his book, How We Think, Dewey (1910) contrasted routine action, based on accumulated habits, with reflective action that is considered, drawing on a combination of experience and consideration of options.

Reflective practice always begins by asking questions such as 'why did I do it like this?' and 'what could I do better next time?'. Whalley calls this 'constructive discontent' (2007, cited in McDowall-Clark and Murray, 2012, p 35), and McDowall-Clark and Murray (2012) suggest that this is the '*catalyst*' (p 35) for improving practice, as opposed to merely criticising it. Reflective practice should therefore be a key characteristic of all early years students, practitioners and leaders.

Schön (1983, cited in Bolton, 2005) developed Dewey's ideas and argued that in a world that is constantly changing, equipping trainee practitioners with knowledge was not enough; they had to be able to adapt their practice appropriately when circumstances changed. Knowing not only *what* action to take in certain situations but *why* that is the best response is key in preventing you from becoming a '*worker-as-technician*' (Moss 2008, cited in Appleby, 2010, p 15) and instead becoming a professional, reflective practitioner.

Schön also introduced the terms '*reflection in action*', referring to the ability to stand outside a situation, observing and considering your actions as they happen in real time, and '*reflection on action*', meaning how you reflect on the action you took after an event (Schön, 1983, cited in Bolton, 2005, p 25). Moon (1999) adds the notion of '*reflection for action*', referring to the way you turn your reflection on action into a change of behaviour. Table 13.1 is an example of a template you may wish to use in order to write down your reflections on your practice.

Table 13.1 Template layout for recording reflections

Date:	What I did:	How I felt:	What would I do differently next time?

As you come to the end of your placement and begin to consider which experiences to draw upon in assignments to show that you can apply theory to practice, taking time to reflect is essential.

Critical questions

» *In your own words describe the differences between a reflective practitioner and a 'worker-as-technician'.*

» *Give some specific examples from your most recent placement of when you have reflected in action, on action and for action.*

The hidden curriculum and ethos

What is meant by the terms '*hidden curriculum*' and '*ethos*'? They can feel a little mysterious because they are not tangible and require reflection and interpretation. They refer to the hidden messages that every setting knowingly or unknowingly conveys and that impact on children's learning as much as the planned curriculum. As you attend different settings, tune into the way the atmosphere makes you feel and record this, as well as the activities that you carry out. When writing about your placement it will demonstrate your awareness that every setting has intangible expectations and culture.

RESEARCH FOCUS

Solvason (2005) conducted some research on culture and ethos and explained that shared meanings, or 'cultural understandings' (Angus, 1998, cited in Solvason, 2005, p 87) are necessary for uniting staff, parents and children. In clarifying the difference between culture and ethos she proposed that:

- culture is found in the structural aspects of a setting, such as the building and contents, school organisation, staff interactions and individual personalities;

- ethos is more elusive and vague, sometimes referred to as 'the mood' of a setting.

The research found that in settings where there is a 'family as opposed to a factory atmosphere' (Acker, 1990, cited in Solvason, 2005, p 88), staff are likely to have high morale, which impacts positively on children's learning (see Chapter 10, Working with colleagues, for further details of how adults' morale influences children's learning).

Critical questions

» Consider and write about the ethos, culture and hidden curriculum you might encounter in each of the following settings:

a) a private school nursery;

b) a committee-run pack away setting;

c) an 80 place, nationally owned 'chain' nursery;

d) a sports centre crèche;

e) a faith school;

f) a children's centre.

Reflective writing

Reflective journals

You have probably heard about the importance of keeping a reflective diary, but might feel that you will remember significant events without the need to write them down. Perhaps you do not enjoy writing and do not want to do any that is not compulsory. However, it is unrealistic to expect that you will remember everything and in the early days of your studies, you may even be unaware of the importance of some events and not register them consciously.

CASE STUDY

Freya

When I began studying, reflection wasn't really something I did; it wasn't until my second year that I started. However, I think it's important in the first year, especially on the foundation degree where a lot of people are new to practice; they might have come in from other areas or just completed level 3, but I think that's the time to be recording anything from practice that stands out because when you come to the second year you can see how you've grown.

You get the high marks when you critically analyse your practice because you talk about your journey, sort of like your own story.

Writing my reflective journal made me more aware of the theory. I'd think 'oh actually, that links to such and such' and that's thinking critically. It's really important that each day you write things that have gone well, things that have not gone so well and ask why.

From descriptive writing to critically analytical writing

As can be seen from Freya's experience, writing a reflective journal requires more than merely describing an event, but continually questioning why.

The following account is repeated three times, each entry becoming successively more reflective.

Planning for JJ: entry 1

For one of my assignments I had to observe a child, plan their next steps based on their interests, carry out the activity and then reflect on what went well and what could be improved. I had done this on a previous placement and felt confident that it would be straight forward. I spent time observing a three year-old boy called JJ. I saw that he liked to carry tools around, but that his hand–eye co-ordination was not very developed.

I borrowed the 'tap-a-shape' from the pre-school room for JJ to try. However, I was disappointed when he did not show any interest in it. I spoke to the room supervisor and she said that I shouldn't worry because since his baby sister was born JJ hadn't concentrated on anything for long. She said I should observe JJ more, noticing how he plays as well as what he plays with.

Critical question

» *This account is descriptive and contains little reflection. See whether you can identify both positive and negative aspects in this account:*

   – *past experiences;*

   – *anticipation of the future;*

- *emotional reaction;*
- *lack of detailed analysis;*
- *ideas presented one at a time and not linked.*

Planning for JJ: entry 2

For one of my assignments I had to observe a child, plan their next steps based on their interests, carry out the activity and then reflect on what went well and what could be improved. I had done something similar during a serial placement at a childminders where I had built a strong bond over a six month period with Sasha, a baby whom I observed every week. Although I knew this time would be slightly different because this placement was a two-week block, I still felt confident that the task would be straight forward.

I spent time making notes on JJ and noticed that he liked carrying a hammer around but did not have well developed hand–eye co-ordination, so I borrowed the 'tap-a-shape' from the pre-school room, thinking that the hammer would attract his attention and hitting the nails would enhance his hand–eye co-ordination.

I felt disappointed and disheartened when JJ did not show any interest in the tap-a-shape. I had thought I was doing well in placement but maybe I'm not as good as I thought. It could be that I was over-confident after the success with Sasha during my previous placement and was too quick to latch on to JJ's attachment to tools which resulted in a superficial response. That'll teach me to not be blasé!

I discussed it with the room leader and I can see that I based my judgement for JJ's next steps on too little information. It would have been better to do different types of observations to try to build a more informed picture of JJ before 'second guessing' his interests. She mentioned that JJ has not concentrated on anything for long since the birth of his baby sister, so perhaps I should have explored this further by talking to JJ's key person and parent.

Critical question

» *This account shows some reflection. See whether you can identify:*

- *consideration, as well as description of the event;*
- *brief analysis;*
- *willingness to be critical of action;*
- *detail, explored where relevant;*
- *some 'standing back' and recognition of the overall effect of the event on the self;*
- *evidence of writing at one point in time, with no acknowledgment that frames of reference can change and affect thinking.*

Planning for JJ: entry 3

For one of my assignments I had to observe a child, plan their next steps based on their interests, carry out the activity and then reflect on what went well and what could be improved. I had done something similar during a serial placement at a childminders where I had built a strong bond over a six month period with Sasha, a baby whom I observed every week. Although I knew this time would be slightly different because this placement was a two week block, I still felt confident that the task would be straight forward.

Looking back I can see that the difference in placement was significant because, whereas I saw Sasha once a week for a six-month period, JJ only attended nursery twice a week. I did not spend time communicating with him but based all my judgements on an observation that he always carried tools around with him. I quickly concluded that by using his interest in the hammer I could enhance his hand–eye co-ordination by encouraging him to hammer nails.

I initially felt disappointed and disheartened when JJ did not show any interest in the tap-a-shape and believe I had become over-confident after the success with Sasha during my previous placement. I might also have been too quick to latch on to JJ's attachment to tools which resulted in a bit of a 'knee-jerk' response of providing tap-a-shape. However, as time has passed and I have talked about it to some of the other students on my course, I can see that this was not an unreasonable conclusion to reach regarding JJ's next steps based on his obvious interest in the tools.

Although the planned activity was not successful, as I write this almost a week after it happened I feel positive that I can learn from this experience; after all, when I am a professional practitioner not everything will run smoothly and I need to get into the habit of reflecting on practice.* It is interesting to see how my perspective of this experience has changed.

I have been wondering what it was about the hammer that was interesting to JJ, if it was not for use as a tool. Perhaps the hammer represented something symbolic. I have undertaken some reading that has made me think – is JJ's attachment to the hammer important to him because it satisfies a need for the power that it represents in a world where he has little power? Qvortrup (2000), when exploring the notion of 'childhood', suggested that it is under attack from the adult world, leaving 'a trade-off between protection and participation, with loss of power to the child' (p 97). Perhaps JJ's need for power has been intensified with the birth of his sibling, which may have made him feel pushed out. Playing with the hammer may be cathartic; Freud (cited in Smidt, 2013) believed that play enabled children to experience control and manage anxieties and I can see that this might be behind JJ's fascination.

Alternatively, it could also be that JJ has spent time with his father in preparing physically for the new baby (building the cot?) which may have made him aware of gender and identity (Smidt, 2013), particularly as the new baby is a girl. Perhaps he is drawn to the hammer as a subconscious way of signifying his masculinity. It may be that he does not feel left out, but a heightened sense of responsibility to protect his mother and sister.

The room leader's suggestion that I spend time talking to JJ,* observing how he plays,* as well as what he plays with,* makes increasing sense. I also need to ask* his key person and mother how he feels about his new sibling, when his interest in tools began and what messages about his position in the family have been given. This will mean I am in a far more informed position to plan JJ's next steps.

This experience has helped me to realise that while two children may display the same behaviour, their motivations may be very different. It is by understanding personal motivations that I will be able to plan in a principled manner that goes beyond tokenism in the future.

*I have used an asterisk to indicate what I will do next to improve.

Critical question

» *This third account shows some deep reflection, incorporating recognition that perspective on an event can change over time. Identify the following features within the passage:*

- *evidence of consideration of different perspectives;*
- *questioning of own assumptions;*
- *recognition that prior experience may have influenced action;*
- *evidence of 'standing back';*
- *a system to divide next steps from reflections;*
- *new learning used to plan further action;*
- *reflection on the way children learn;*
- *evidence of relating theory to practice, including references;*
- *evidence of self as developing practitioner.*

(All prompts based on ideas presented by Moon, 2001)

Structure and style

You might be so enthusiastic about your placement experience that you are tempted to write about all the interesting things that have happened to you. However, to select the most relevant experiences, try to identify themes that link your experiences, outlining them in the introduction and then addressing them systematically in your writing. At certain intervals, briefly review your reflections and conclusions so far and then introduce the next theme. Check the learning outcomes or marking criteria, making it clear how each of the themes are relevant.

SMART targets

When writing a self-improvement action plan there are certain criteria that need to be applied to ensure its appropriateness. The acronym 'SMART' is often used as a way of remembering how to construct useful targets:

Specific – what exactly are you going to do?

Measureable – how will you know when your target has been achieved?

Achievable – with the resources you have to work with

Realistic – targets should stretch you but within accepted limitations

Timebound – within a specific timeframe

For examples of what you may want to include in an action plan see Appendix 2 – Self-assessment audit of skills and knowledge – at the end of the book.

Chapter reflections

This chapter has focused on the transition between the hustle and bustle of placement to beginning to make sense of your experiences. Developing into a reflective practitioner, looking beyond the obvious and persistently asking 'why?' may feel a little unnatural at first, but children need practitioners who wonder about how they learn and how they can be helped to learn more. This is why it is worth taking the time to slow down sometimes, and just reflect. Reflecting on key learning moments from your placement experience will ensure that you are not only effective in practice but are rewarded with high marks in assignments as well.

Further reading

Hayes, C, Daley, J, Duncan, M, Gill, R and Whitehouse, A (2014) *Developing as a Reflective Early Years Professional.* Northwich: Critical Publishing.

References

Appleby, K (2010) Reflective Thinking, Reflective Practice, in Reed, M and Canning, N (eds) *Reflective Practice in the Early Years*. London: Sage.

Bolton, G (2005) *Reflective Practice, Writing and Professional Development* (2nd edition). London: Sage.

Dewey, J (1910) *How We Think*. New York: DC Hearth.

McDowall-Clark, R and Murray, J (2012) *Reconceptualizing Leadership in the Early Years*. Maidenhead: Open University Press.

Moon, J (1999) *Reflection in Learning and Professional Development*. London: Kogan Paul.

Moon. J (2001) *PDP Working Paper 4 Reflection in Higher Education Learning*. Itsn Generic Centre. [online] Available at: www.york.ac.uk/admin/hr/researcher-development/students/resources/pgwt/reflectivepractice.pdf (accessed 1 December 2014).

Qvortrup, J (2000) Microanalysis of Childhood, in Christensen, P and James, A (eds) *Research With Children, Perspectives and Practices*. London: Falmer Press, pp 77–97.

Smidt, S (2013) *The Developing Child in the 21st Century: A global perspective on child development*. Oxon: Routledge.

Solvason, C (2005) Investigating Specialist School Ethos … Or Do You Mean Culture?, *Education Studies*, 31(1): 85–94.

Appendix 1

Teachers' Standards (Early Years) September 2013

1.   **Set high expectations which inspire, motivate and challenge all children.**

   1.1   Establish and sustain a safe and stimulating environment where children feel confident and are able to learn and develop.

   1.2   Set goals that stretch and challenge children of all backgrounds, abilities and dispositions.

   1.3   Demonstrate and model the positive values, attitudes and behaviours expected of children.

2.   **Promote good progress and outcomes by children.**

   2.1   Be accountable for children's progress, attainment and outcomes.

   2.2   Demonstrate knowledge and understanding of how babies and children learn and develop.

   2.3   Know and understand attachment theories, their significance and how effectively to promote secure attachments.

   2.4   Lead and model effective strategies to develop and extend children's learning and thinking, including sustained shared thinking.

   2.5   Communicate effectively with children from birth to age five, listening and responding sensitively.

   2.6   Develop children's confidence, social and communication skills through group learning.

   2.7   Understand the important influence of parents and/or carers, working in partnership with them to support the child's well-being, learning and development.

3.   **Demonstrate good knowledge of early learning and EYFS.**

   3.1   Have a secure knowledge of early childhood development and how that leads to successful learning and development at school.

   3.2   Demonstrate a clear understanding of how to widen children's experience and raise their expectations.

3.3 Demonstrate a critical understanding of the EYFS areas of learning and development and engage with the educational continuum of expectations, curricula and teaching of Key Stage 1 and 2.

3.4 Demonstrate a clear understanding of systematic synthetic phonics in the teaching of early reading.

3.5 Demonstrate a clear understanding of appropriate strategies in the teaching of early mathematics.

4. **Plan education and care taking account of the needs of all children.**

4.1 Observe and assess children's development and learning, using this to plan next steps.

4.2 Plan balanced and flexible activities and educational programmes that take into account the stage of development, circumstances and interests of children.

4.3 Promote a love of learning and stimulate children's intellectual curiosity in partnership with parents and/or carers.

4.4 Use a variety of teaching approaches to lead group activities appropriate to the age range and ability of children.

4.5 Reflect on the effectiveness of teaching activities and educational programmes to support the continuous improvement of provision.

5. **Adapt education and care to respond to the strengths and needs of all children.**

5.1 Have a secure understanding of how a range of factors can inhibit children's learning and development and how best to address these.

5.2 Demonstrate an awareness of the physical, emotional, social, intellectual development and communication needs of babies and children, and know how to adapt education and care to support children at different stages of development.

5.3 Demonstrate a clear understanding of the needs of all children, including those with special educational needs and disabilities, and be able to use and evaluate distinctive approaches to engage and support them.

5.4 Support children through a range of transitions.

5.5 Know when a child is in need of additional support and how this can be accessed, working in partnership with parents and/or carers and other professionals.

6. **Make accurate and productive use of assessment.**

6.1 Understand and lead assessment within the framework of the EYFS, including statutory assessment requirements (see annex 1).

6.2 Engage effectively with parents and/or carers and other professionals in the on-going assessment and provision for each child.

6.3 Give regular feedback to children and parents and/or carers to help children progress towards their goals.

7. **Safeguard and promote the welfare of children, and provide a safe learning environment.**

7.1 Know and act upon the legal requirements and guidance on health and safety, safeguarding and promoting the welfare of the child.

7.2 Establish and sustain a safe environment and employ practices that promote children's health and safety.

7.3 Know and understand child protection policies and procedures, recognise when a child is in danger or at risk of abuse, and know how to act to protect them.

8. **Fulfil wider professional responsibilities.**

8.1 Promote equality of opportunity and anti-discriminatory practice.

8.2 Make a positive contribution to the wider life and ethos of the setting.

8.3 Take a lead in establishing a culture of co-operative working between colleagues, parents and/or carers and other professionals.

8.4 Model and implement effective education and care, and support and lead other practitioners including Early Years Educators.

8.5 Take responsibility for leading practice through appropriate professional development for self and colleagues.

8.6 Reflect on and evaluate the effectiveness of provision, and shape and support good practice.

8.7 Understand the importance of and contribute to multi-agency team working.

Appendix 2

Self-assessment audit of skills and knowledge

Name: ....

Student Number: ....

Level: ....

Semester: ....

Skill	Range of skills	Health and safety considerations	Theory and knowledge related to the skills	Date achieved
1. Infant nutrition options	• Preparation of infant feed formula; • Sterilisation of bottles; • Storage of expressed breast milk; • Bottle-feeding babies.			
2. Baby weaning	• Introduction to solid foods; • Baby-led weaning.			

Skill	Range of skills	Health and safety considerations	Theory and knowledge related to the skills	Date achieved
3. Healthy eating for young children	• Provision of food that meets government policy for children's healthy eating; • Provision of food for children with medical dietary needs; • Provision of food for children with cultural requirements; • Supervision of snacks and meals for young children; • Access for toddlers and children to fluids.			
4. Toilet needs of children	• Changing a nappy; • Privacy and safeguarding issues; • Introducing toilet training; • Supervision of children visiting the toilet.			
5. Hygiene needs of children	• Hand hygiene; • Care of hair; • Dental hygiene.			

Skill	Range of skills	Health and safety considerations	Theory and knowledge related to the skills	Date achieved
6. Dressing and undressing children	• Promoting independence; • Encouraging fine motor skill development.			
7. Communication with parents/ carers	• Introduce self to parents/carers; • Learn the names of parents; • Write in home/ setting diary; • Share something positive about a child with their parent/carer; • Open the door to parents in the morning to welcome them into the setting.			
8. Be a shadow key person	• Negotiate a child to share with a key person; • Contribute to planning for the child; • Observe the child and suggest next steps drawing on theory and the child's interests; • Contribute to a child's learning journey; • Observe a two year-old check.			

Skill	Range of skills	Health and safety considerations	Theory and knowledge related to the skills	Date achieved
9. Lead an activity with a larger group of children	• Read a story to a small group of children; • Plan and carry out an activity with a group of children both indoors and outdoors; • Plan and carry out an activity with a large group of children/the whole class.			
10. Relationships with staff	• Introduce self to staff; • Learn staff names; • Attend a planning / staff meeting.			
11. Enabling environment	• Negotiate a display board space; • Display an aspect of the work you have done with children; • Include the child's voice; • Make it interactive; • Add links to show parents how it relates to the EYFS prime and/or specific areas.			

Skill	Range of skills	Health and safety considerations	Theory and knowledge related to the skills	Date achieved
12. Plan an off-site visit	• Do a risk assessment; • Ensure correct ratios as stated in the EYFS; • Make appropriate contacts; • Inform parents.			
13. Make/ introduce a resource	• Observe children's interests and add a resource to extend the continuous provision; • Evaluate the resource.			
14. Work with a child with special educational needs	• Negotiate with the manager; • Take part in agreed interventions; • Contribute to an Individualized Education Program (IEP); • Work with a professional from outside the setting.			
15. Support transitions	• Help a new child settle in; • Help a child move from room to room; • Help parents and children in the preparation for school.			

Skill	Range of skills	Health and safety considerations	Theory and knowledge related to the skills	Date achieved
16. Support safeguarding	• Complete safeguarding training; • Complete an accident on arrival sheet; • Complete an accident in the setting sheet; • Review the accident sheets to look for significant trends; • Learn who to contact in a whistleblowing situation if you cannot go to the manager.			
17. Engage with the ethos of the setting	• Join in with a fundraising activity; • Help with an open day or parents' event.			

Index

adjourning, 90
Allen, G, 46
Athey, C, 61
attachment theory, 65

Bowlby, J, 60, 65, 105
Bruce, T, 62
Bruner, J, 60

case studies
    Climbié, Victoria, 34
    comment on, 63
    Little Stars Nursery, 30
    Little Teds Nursery, 31–2
    practitioner views, 25
    pre-placement visit, 12
    sustained shared thinking, 78–80
    two year-old check, 83
child development
    chronic/complex medical need, 64
    context and environment, 63
    cultural expectations, 64
    minor illness, 64
    special educational needs, 64
child protection, 28
childminding, 20
Children Act 1989, 29, 46
Children Act 2004, 29
chronic/complex medical needs, 64
Climbié, Victoria, 34
communication, 8, 129
communities of practice, 21
continuing professional development, 19
cultural unease, 93

DBS, see Disclosure and Barring Service
Development Matters, 70, 84
Dewey, J, 115
Disclosure and Barring Service (DBS), 33
documents
    age of opportunity, 44
    Allen report, 41
    EPPE project, 37
    Every Child Matters, 46
    Field Report, 39
    Marmot Review, 39

Monro Review, 46
Nutbrown Review, 42
supporting families, 41
UNCRC, 46
Donaldson, M, 60

early childhood education and care (ECEC)
    grand thinkers, 59
    placement preparation, 6
    theory in, 58
Early Years Foundation Stage (EYFS), 29, 65
Early Years Foundation Stage Profile (EYFSP)
    case study, 84
    research focus, 84
    summary of check, 84
Early Years Professional Status (EYPS), 18
early years professionalism, 21
early years settings, 5, 6
Early Years Teacher Status (EYTS), 18
ECEC, see early childhood education and care
Effective Provision of Pre-School Education (EPPE) project,
    37, 70, 78
emotional transition management, 114
ethical relationships, student responsibilities, 106
ethical responsibility, 54
ethos, 116, 117
event sampling, 74
Every Child Matters, 29, 46
EYFSP, see Early Years Foundation Stage Profile
EYPS, see Early Years Professional Status
EYTS, see Early Years Teacher Status

Field report, 39
Field, F, 46
first day, see planning goals; professional responsibilities
first impressions, 51–2
flow, 71
forming, 90
Freud, S, 60
Froebel, F, 59

goals, see planning goals
good enough parenting, 99
grand thinkers, 59

hidden curriculum, 116

informal learning, 55
initiative, 53
Isaacs, S, 60, 70

Laevers, F, 71
legislation
 relationship with children, 105
 safeguarding, 29–33
Leuven Scale for Involvement, 72–3
long-term planning, 76

male practitioners, 93
Marmot Review, 39
Marmot, M, 39
Maslow's hierarchy of needs, 91
medium-term planning, 76
minor illness, 64
modern theorists, 61
Monro Review, 46
Montessori, M, 60

narrative observation, 74
NMC, see Nursing and Midwifery Council
NNEB, see Nursery Nurse Examination Board
norming, 90
Nursery Nurse Examination Board (NNEB), 17
Nursing and Midwifery Council (NMC), 19
Nutbrown Review, 1, 7, 42
Nutbrown, C, 18, 42

observation
 checklist method, 74
 description, 73
 event sampling, 74
 narrative, 74
 planning and assessment with, 70
 rating scale, 74
 time sampling, 74
 tracking, 74
Ofsted, 7
outstanding, Ofsted rating, 7

Page, J, 109
partnership, 98, 99, vii
Pascal, C, 22
pedagogy, vii
performing, 90
Piaget, J, 19, 59, 60, 70
placement preparation
 communication settings, 8
 contact via email, 9
 early years settings, 5, 6
 good/outstanding Ofsted rating, 7
 keeping yourself well, 11–12
 learning opportunities, 13
 professional conduct, 12
 researching suitable settings, 7
 selection of settings, 5

planning
 individual needs, 74–5
 Leuven Scale for Involvement, 72–3
 long-term, 76
 medium-term, 76
 observation and assessment with, 70
 process/product, 76–8
 short-term, 76
planning goals
 capturing informal learning, 55
 description, 53
 ethical issues, 54
 practical skills, 53
policy and practice theory, 65–6
practice-based learning, see work-based
 learning (WBL)
practitioner as theorist, 61
pre-placement visit, 10
professional conduct, 12
professional educator
 description, 21
 placement approach, 24
 research focus, 23
professional register, 19
professional responsibilities
 finding position, 52
 first impressions, 51–2
 initiative, 53
 policies, 52
professionalism
 body of knowledge and research, 19
 continuing professional development, 19
 definition, 16
 early years, 21
 entry restrictions to occupation, 18
 features of, 16–21
 leadership, 20
 pay and status, 20
 professional register, 19
 standards and code of conduct, 21
 training and education, 17–18

rating scale, 74
reflection for action, 116
reflection in action, 116
reflective integrity, 93
reflective journals, 117–18
reflective practice, 115
reflective writing
 critical analysis, 118–21
 reflective journals, 117–18
 SMART style, 122
 structure and style, 121
relationship with children
 ethical, 106
 interacting with toddlers in practice, 108–9
 interaction with young children in practice, 109–10
 interactions with babies in practice, 107–8

legislation, policy and research, 105
role of key person, 105

safeguarding
being suitable person, 33
definition, 28
knowledge of factors, 33
legislation and policy, 29–33
policies in settings, 30
whistleblowing policy, 30
Schön, D, 115
SCRs, *see* serious case reviews
self-assessment audit, skills and knowledge, 127
serious case reviews (SCRs)
Little Stars Nursery, 30
Little Teds Nursery, 31–2
short-term planning, 76
Skinner, B, 60
SMART targets, 122
social networking, 32
special educational needs, 64
Steiner, R, 60
storming, 90
summative assessment
Early Years Foundation Stage Profile, 84–5
two year-old check, 82–4
supporting families document, 41
sustained shared thinking, 78–80

targeted plan, 82
team development theory, 90
theorists
grand thinkers, 59
modern, 61
practitioner as, 61
theory
attachment, 65
child development, 63–4
creation of, 58
defining in ECEC, 58
importance of, 61

policy and practice, 65–6
team development, 90
Tickell, D C, 46, 84
time sampling, 74
tracking, observational strategy, 74
two year-old check
case study, 83
research focus, 82
summary of check, 82

UNCRC, *see* United Nations Convention on the
Rights of the Child
United Nations Convention on the Rights of
the Child (UNCRC), 29, 46

Vygotsky, L, 60, 78

Wave Trust, 66
WBL, *see* work-based learning
Whariki, T, 99
whistleblowing policy, 30
Winnicott, D, 99
work-based learning (WBL), 1
Working Together to Safeguard Children
guidance, 29
working with colleagues
importance of relationship, 88
male practitioners, 93
Maslow's hierarchy of needs, 91
problems during placement, 93
successful relationships, 92
working with parents
all kinds of families, 98
fostering well-being, 99
good enough parenting, 99
implications for placement, 101–2
research focus, 97
role of key person, 99
shared dialogue, 100

zone of proximal development, 78